# EXCEPTIONAL NOT EXPECTED

## An Ordinary Woman's Guide to Living an Empowered Life

### VOLUME 2

Author

Yvonne Ellis

www.yemeempowerment.com

Yvonne Ellis/Exceptional Not Expected

ISBN:978-1-9998590-5-3

Photo credit for Exceptional Not Expected Volume 1 and 2 Jada Ellis

# DEDICATION

Thank you, Father God, for the gift of ideas, wisdom, knowledge, and inner standing. You are the bread of life.

To my husband, Stephen, I hope my book inspires you to be exceptional.

My darling Jada, I love you forever and always my love.

Tennika you are never far from my thoughts. I love you.

Carline, thank you for your mentorship and encouragement.

To all those seeking to live an empowered life. This book is for you.

# Contents (50)

# Introduction

Welcome to volume two of *Exceptional, Not Expected.*

Despite being the author of this series, I continue to reflect on the wisdom and lessons I have learned from my life experiences thus far. There have been real testing moments on my journey to live an exceptional and not unexpected life. The main test, is not only to apply and live out my gained knowledge, but also to continue to motivate myself to strive towards the standard of person I want to be.

Sometimes, when recurring challenges emerge in my life, I wonder how God (my Father and teacher) will grade my efforts in handling them. Will I pass the test, or will I have to try again? Am I doing what is expected of me, or am I striving to be exceptional? I am reminded of the school report of my—then fourteen-year-old—daughter's educational attainment at school (she is now at university) which inspired the Exceptional Not Expected books. Her school report listed the subjects she had undertaken, and her teachers graded her learning comprehension of each subject as follows: expected (basically means as predicted) and exceptional (exceeded expectations). Some of my greatest life tests have included subjects such as overcoming the trauma of childhood sexual abuse, staying faithful to God and true to myself, being reflective, not reactive to negative situations, holding onto hope and faith when situations look bleak, all whilst developing a mindset to develop personally, despite circumstances. It has not been easy. When the tests and trials come (and they always do), I try to use what I have already learned with wisdom to overcome whatever current challenge I face, knowing that my teacher (God) is encouraging me to pass.

It is slightly tempting in challenging moments to retreat to the default position of a long time ago, where the comfort zone of living expected and predicted, was a nice place to be. However, when I reflect on how far I have come since the age of thirty-five when I started this journey, I am encouraged and inspired by my progress and the changes within me. Years of personal development work have shaped who I am today, and I'm proud of the courage it took to live a life that's Exceptional not Expected. I continue to push forward.

In this book, *Exceptional Not Expected: An Ordinary Woman's Guide to Living an Empowered Life, Volume Two,* I continue to share with you my knowledge, advice, wisdom, tips, encouragement, and insight, from going through different experiences. It is empowering knowledge which I have shared in part through blogs, podcasts, social media posts, and countless journal notes I have kept over the years; reflections continuously gathered from my life journey. I talk about various subjects. Some of the entries are long and detailed, and others are short and to the point. Nonetheless, all that I share from my journey in this book has contributed to my personal success. Additionally, throughout the book, I have included quotes that I created to empower, encourage, and inspire you. You can read this book from start to finish, start with an entry that resonates with you the most, or go directly to the subject matter for the situation you are facing. I also share a biblical word to encourage you. Even though I see myself as exceptional, I am no different to you. I started from where I was with what I had. I changed my life from what was expected, and you can too!

Yvonne x

# What You Can Do with Imagination Is Limitless

*YEME Empowerment*

# A Birthday Reminder

How do you feel about your birthday? The arrival of another birthday often stirs mixed emotions in many people. For some, it serves as a reminder of ageing, while for others, it highlights the goals they have yet to achieve. Beyond the mixed feelings, birthdays should be seen as a time not just for celebration, but also for reflection.

When I celebrated my 48th birthday, I kept the day low-key. However, I spent the days leading up to it, as I do every year, in deep reflection. My birthday offers me a chance to assess my life goals, consider any challenges I'm facing, and evaluate where I stand emotionally, mentally, and spiritually. This introspection isn't limited to just my birthday; it's a practice I've maintained for the past twenty years through journaling. Every few years, I revisit these journals, and it's always a delight to see how much progress I've made; the challenges that once seemed insurmountable have been overcome, and goals I once doubted have been achieved. I'm always reminded of the Bible verse, *"Being confident of this very thing, that He who began a good work in you will carry it on to completion until the day of Christ Jesus"* (**Philippians 1:6**).

After much reflection, I find peace in where I am on this birthday. Despite the challenges of life, I recognise that I have much to be grateful for. Each new day is a blessing and a reminder that as long as I have the gift of time, the opportunity to pursue my goals and dreams remains. As I step into a new year of life (because I truly believe that each new age marks a new year), I will focus on self-improvement, continue to build courage by embracing new experiences, and always remain thankful to God for the opportunity to do so.

No matter how you feel about your birthday, I encourage you to take a moment to focus on the positive things you've achieved in your life thus far. In the days leading up to your special day, choose three things to remind yourself of, as you step into the new year of your life. If you're struggling to come up with ideas, here are three reminders to inspire you:

**Be kind to yourself**

Allow yourself grace when you make mistakes or face challenges you are yet to overcome. Self-compassion is key.

**Life is a journey**

Embrace it. Be patient with yourself and appreciate the lessons each moment offers. It's through this journey that you'll grow into the person you're meant to be. Trust that everything will unfold in God's perfect timing.

**Trust in the Lord**

I'm reminded that trying to figure everything out on my own rarely goes as planned. Reflecting on my past, I see that I never had all the answers—God did and still does. I am learning to let go of my tendency to worry and choose to trust in the Lord, not lean on my own understanding. I encourage you to do the same **(Proverbs 3:5).**

I hope your birthday serves as a joyful reminder of just how far you've come and how much you've accomplished.

*For through wisdom, your days will be many, and years will be added to your life.* **Proverbs 9:11**

# A Setback Is a Set-Up for a Great Comeback

There are many situations in life that can set you back. However, in my experience, I have found that setbacks are a setup for a great comeback. Let me share with you some things that set me back: childhood sexual abuse trauma (22 years). Depression and anxiety (20 years). Unexpected life change and loss (immeasurable). At the time of going through each of these experiences, I thought the setbacks were final. I felt that I was taking one step forward and ten steps back. I became frustrated at times with the setbacks. I felt that time was passing me by. I believed my best years were behind me, because aren't the best years your younger years? My childhood was ruined by abuse. My teen years were spent struggling with trauma, depression, and finding my way as a single parent; my twenties battling with depression and self-esteem issues, and my thirties—well… they were spent trying to figure out who I was, and where my life was going. I spent so much time focusing on the loss and setbacks that I didn't see the bigger picture of what was unfolding in my life. Amazing things were happening to me during this time. Each setback taught me something as I reflected on it. I thought about what caused the setback and what I could do differently the next time. I became resilient. Rather than cry and give up when challenges that caused each setback came, they made me stronger—and I bounced back quicker.

Newfound maturity started to develop within me, because I changed my mindset and perspective about how I viewed setbacks. Fast forward to today: I realise that the setbacks were my *setup* for the success I have today. I am stronger, wiser, and better for experiencing them. Furthermore, those setbacks have empowered me and served as teaching moments that I use to encourage and empower others through the many skills, talents, and experiences God has blessed me with. I just want to encourage you. If you are going through things that you consider setbacks, please remember, **setbacks are not final**. Use your time during the setback, to set you up better than you ever have before, by:

**Developing yourself**

In what you consider a setback, ask yourself: what can I improve or do differently? Don't waste time being frustrated. Instead, do something that will empower you in the situation.

## Keeping focused on the goal

Setbacks can cause you to forget that once you have overcome them, there is a destination to reach. Use the time to keep acquainted with your goal. Inspire and motivate yourself with things that will keep hope alive in your heart and help you believe that, in due time, you will achieve your goal.

## Remembering that a setback is never final

The only thing that is final is if you choose to give up. Remember: setbacks are just challenges in a period of time to allow you to prepare for better things in your future.

*You are of God, little children, and have overcome them, because He who is in you is greater than he who is in the world.* **1 John 4:4**

# Bad Habits Don't Make
# You a Bad Person

It is easy to condemn yourself when you cannot break your bad habits. You have tried everything in your own strength to stop whatever you are doing, but you end up failing miserably, and because of your inability to overcome your habit, you think it makes you a bad person. Here is the truth: You are NOT a bad person. You are just caught up in some things that are not good for you. I know what it is like to be caught up in bad habits. It can make you feel defeated and discouraged, but there is hope.

First of all, you need to understand that habits take time to break. Habits need personal determination and unwavering supportive strength that needs to come from a source other than yourself (Jesus). Also, you need to not condemn yourself whilst in the process of trying to get free from your habit. You need patience on the journey to break from your habit. When you feel condemned because of your habit or addiction, remember that God is a forgiving and merciful God. Jesus, his son, can deliver you from the stronghold your habit has over you and your life and help you. Here are some things that I am using to help me break bad habits:

## Make a way out plan ahead of time to deal with your habit

You see the ditch up ahead in the road. You know that if you do not take an alternative route, you will fall into it. What can you do to avoid falling into the same habit today? How can you divert your attention away from it? Don't wait until you are in the ditch to think about it. Plan ahead so you can at least try and avoid falling into it.

## Replace it with something different

I spent too much time and effort focusing on and engaging in my bad habit. I realised that I needed to spend my energy getting back into the habit of doing things I love (reading, writing, content creation). Pursuing these outlets again has helped me to focus on healthier things, which I enjoy. Think about one alternative thing you can do when the urge to engage in your habit arises.

## Show yourself grace

Remember, no one is perfect. At least you can acknowledge and accept that you need to change the things you are doing. Self-condemnation is not going to help you overcome your habit. Be kind to yourself on your journey to being an overcomer.

*Bless the Lord, O my soul, and not forget all his benefits: Who forgives all your iniquities, who heals all your diseases* **Psalm 103:2-3**

# Ballet Dreams

Towards the end of 2024, I visited the Royal Opera and Ballet House in Covent Garden. This experience had long been on my "Dream List". To my delight, I got to check it off much sooner than I expected. One morning, I googled the Royal Opera House and discovered they were hosting a free exhibition called *Pioneers of Black British Ballet*. Intrigued, I decided to see it for myself.

Nestled in a quiet corner of the Ballet and Opera House, the exhibition carried an understated tone, despite the profound significance of the journeys each of these Black ballerinas undertook to realise their dreams. Among them, Brenda Garratt-Glassman's story stood out as a shining beacon of inspiration; marking her as the first Black female student at the Royal Ballet Upper School.

Brenda was born in 1955 to Guyanese parents. She began her dance training at the Joyce Butler School of Dance at the age of eight. While many encouraged her to pursue a career in cabaret performance, Butler recognised her exceptional talent and foresaw the challenges Brenda would face due to racial barriers in her home country. At 16, Brenda performed for an audience that included the director of the Royal

Academy of Dance, who was so impressed that they invited her to audition for the Royal Ballet School. This led to her becoming the first Black student. However, Brenda was told she would not be hired by the principal company because of her race.

Brenda encountered countless challenges on her path to fulfilling her dream of becoming a ballerina. In the fiercely competitive world of dance, many tried to limit her potential, suggesting that she pursue contemporary dance instead. Despite her undeniable talent, some dismissed her aspirations, deeming her dream of becoming a ballerina unrealistic.

But Brenda refused to let the doubts and limitations imposed by others deter her. Her powerful motto, *"No matter what anyone says, know your worth; you are already enough,"* was born from her struggles with those who judged her not on her skill, creativity, or talent, but on the colour of her skin. Choosing to rise above the negativity, she placed unwavering faith in herself and her abilities, proving that belief in one's worth is one of the essential cornerstones of success.

The story of Brenda Garratt Glassman's *ballet dreams,* offers valuable lessons, inspiration, and encouragement that can resonate with anyone striving to achieve a dream:

## People will put barriers on your dream

Many people tend to fear, dismiss, or doubt what they don't understand—especially when they believe they've already defined your potential. Unfortunately, others may project their limitations onto you. That's why it's essential to be mindful of who you share your dreams with, particularly in the early stages. Don't give others the chance to diminish your aspirations before you've even begun pursuing them. While you'll undoubtedly face personal challenges, don't let others create additional hurdles along your journey.

## Dreams take time

Brenda had cherished her dream since the age of eight. Her passion for dance was unwavering, and in 1985, she defied the odds by achieving what many said was impossible: becoming the principal ballet dancer in *Maiden*. But ask yourself: would you commit to pursuing a dream for twenty years? Most would abandon it. Only a determined few persevere. Chasing a dream requires more than ambition—it demands time, dedication, and patience. The journey is a process of growth, skill refinement, and accumulating experience. Sometimes, success also hinges on external factors that work in your favour. The key is to cultivate a mindset that embraces patience as an essential part of fulfilment of your dream.

**Believe in yourself when your dream takes you into unknown territory**

Pursuing any dream is challenging, but when that dream doesn't fit society's expectations, or when others try to define who you should be or where you belong, the struggle intensifies. Yet, this is often part of the journey, especially when you are venturing into the unknown. The key to overcoming these obstacles is to develop self-belief and stay focused. A strong sense of belief in yourself will drown out the voices that try to oppose you. Furthermore, having a clear vision of your dream will help keep the path in focus, even when challenges arise.

The saying "nothing good comes easy" is undoubtedly true. I'm still learning that lesson every day. Even though I've been on this journey for six years, the dreams I'm chasing still demand sacrifice, dedication, motivation, and unwavering belief in their possibility. Yet, the pursuit of Brenda's ballet dreams mirrors the journey of all dreamers. There's nothing to lose, and so much to gain, if we hold on to the dreams in our hearts. Even when things seem tough, don't lose hope. Trust that one day, your dreams will come true. The reward will make every challenge worth it.

*Jesus looked at them and said, "With man this is impossible, but with God all things are possible."* **Matthew 19:26**

# Be Yourself

The main thing that you need to live an exceptional and not expected life, is to be yourself. Far too many people live for the approval, opinion, and validation of others. This is especially evident on social media, where the court of public opinion overrides the liberty to think independently of the crowd. We live in a day and age where people will try to cancel you for not following popular or mass opinion. Long before mainstream cancel culture, people were pressured to follow certain cultural, career, and life paths within their family or community. Without a firm foundation of self, it can be hard to resist the influence of outside factors. That is why I believe it is important to have a foundation rooted in God, from whom personal identity, purpose, and vision originate. In planting myself in God, I discovered my true self and what my life purpose is. After finally finding myself in my thirties, after childhood abuse, I promised to live my life authentically and be free to be myself. I hope you are living life in this way, too.

It is okay to be you. We are not made or meant to be the same. You don't have to be the same as other people, you don't have to like what other people like, have the same opinions, or do what others are doing. That is the beauty of life and the gift of freewill from the Living God that we have the liberty to be ourselves. Ultimately, you are responsible for your life and the choices and decisions you make. One day you will, the same as I, give an account for the life we have been given. But don't be afraid to live your life. Don't be afraid to be you and stand in your individuality that God gave you. If you struggle with being yourself, you can:

**Discover yourself**

Get to know who you are. Discover your likes and dislikes. Find out what makes you tick, what brings you joy, and what things make you uniquely you. The journey to being yourself can take a lifetime, and that is okay as long as you uncover who you authentically are and embrace it.

**Stand true to you**

People without a stable foundation of who they are can be easily swayed into someone they are not. It takes real confidence to stand true to yourself when most people are doing the same thing. It can cause feelings of fear of rejection or make you second-guess your opinions, choices, and who you are.

**Celebrate your strengths**

Rather than focus on your shortcomings or the things you would like to change celebrate your strengths.

Celebrate the things that are uniquely you. Are you strong-minded? Celebrate it. Able to know the things you enjoy in life? celebrate. Are you a person of good character with morals? celebrate. Even if there is one thing or ten things, acknowledge each and every thing that makes you uniquely you.

*Yet you, Lord, are our Father. We are the clay; you are the potter; we are all the work of your hand.* **Isaiah 64:8**

# Be Your Own Cheerleader

One of the things I talk about in my third book, *Into the Unknown,* is that one of the most important things you must learn if you want to live exceptional and not expected, is to be your own cheerleader. Of course, it would be nice if someone were on the sidelines cheering you on as you attempt new things in your life, but this is rarely the case, especially when you are doing things that other people are not doing, or doing things they don't understand.

I know from experience how hard and discouraging it can be to discover that your loved ones don't support your courageous audacity to break out from the old to try something new, but when you taste the freedom of living life doing the things you once dreamt you never thought you could do, feeling happy, peaceful and living with meaning, it compensates for the lack of encouragement of others. There is an important requirement, though; you must be your own cheerleader. You must motivate yourself and find inspiration to encourage *you* on your journey to living your dreams. You can become your own cheerleader by:

## Find cheerleading content

Listen to podcasts, interviews, and read books from people who have done things you are attempting to do. This is crucial, especially if you do not have anyone around you who is doing similar things. I found great encouragement in podcasts such as the Bold Idea podcast with Leary O Gates and Amin Assadi. Also reading books like The Magic of Thinking Big by David Schultz, Slight Edge by Jeff Olson and Embrace the Struggle, by Zig Ziglar. Fill your mind with empowering content, and it does wonders for cheerleading you.

## Celebrate your wins, success, and achievements

Celebration should be your reward for the great things you are doing. It does not matter if anyone else does not think your efforts are worth acknowledging. As long as you acknowledge your hard work, that is all that matters. In doing so, it will motivate you to continue and remember the 'why' during the times you may want to give up.

## Allow your aspirations to encourage you

This will build your confidence and self-belief. Also, put yourself in environments that inspire and encourage you. Everything starts with you. Anything after that is a bonus. Learn to be your own cheerleader and find a way to cheer yourself on today.

*Be strong and of good courage, do not fear nor be afraid of them; for the Lord your God, He is the One who goes with you. He will not leave you nor forsake you."* **Deuteronomy 31:6**

# Be Willing to Do Something Different

Have you heard the saying: 'do the same thing, expect the same results'?

It does sound bizarre that someone would keep doing the same thing, knowing that the outcome of their action will bring the same predicted results. But that can easily happen because of habits, lack of knowledge of the thing they want to change, not knowing how to make a change for different results, or even naively believing that one day the issue, problem, or challenge will somehow change by itself without any influence or input from them.

If you find yourself on a repetitive hamster wheel of endless same outcomes, you need to know you are the instigator for change. No matter the circumstances, you must be willing to do something different. Your willingness to disrupt the norm triggers the change process, and it will help you to seek out new things to empower you to make the changes. From personal experience, I know this is not easy to do. It is hard to make changes to things you have been used to doing for so long. However, everybody has a breaking point. It is that place of being 'sick and tired' and fed up with being fed up. And you will know it when you reach it. It is the day you hate doing the same thing. You will find yourself resenting it, and will keep thinking 'I want to change this thing, but I can't change it'. However, I want to encourage you; the fact that you feel like this means you are indeed at the point of being willing to do something different. You just need to know how. It is important to take advantage of this desire by:

## Considering what you would be willing to try

For example, you are overweight and struggle to exercise. You hate going to the gym, but would you be willing to try walking? The point is, you are willing to try *something* different. This should be the focus. Everything else can be worked on over time. Whatever the thing is that you are stuck with, consider an alternative you are willing to try.

## Be intentional

You must be intentional in doing something different. It won't be easy to go against the routine of things you are used to. It will require you to focus on the new, different thing you have added to your life and to be aware of things that keep you in a repetitive cycle.

## Don't write yourself off

This is crucial to remember. Don't resign yourself to the belief that you are stuck in ways, or that you cannot change ingrained habits. If you have the desire to be willing to do something different, change is closer than you think.

*The heart of the prudent acquires knowledge, And the ear of the wise seeks knowledge.* **Proverbs 18:15**

# Brain Overload

Have you ever experienced brain overload? You know the feeling: when your brain is overwhelmed with juggling numerous thoughts simultaneously. Additionally, it's compounded by the constant stimulation from TV, social media, and the competing demands battling for your attention from people, tasks, and other everyday obligations. If you can relate, isn't it overwhelming?

I went through a period of severe brain overload. After two years of rigorous studying for my master's degree, alongside work commitments, managing family responsibilities, engaging in social media content creation, and maintaining a constant stream of activities, I found it increasingly challenging to keep focused. Also, I noticed a decline in my energy levels and there were times where I struggled to stay asleep. I believe these signs are indicative of brain overload and have become apparent to me. Other brain overload indicators can include:

- Struggling to maintain focus on or complete a task in time.

- Easily distracted.

- Lack of enthusiastic energy to work towards or complete goals.

- Overanxious or excessive worry about life situations.
- Overwhelmed with too many thoughts.

In our roles as women—whether as mothers, career professionals, caregivers, or community supporters, we can often find ourselves grappling with brain overload and consider it okay. Multitasking is often hailed as a defining female trait, which is an outward expression of our continuous mental activity and engagement. Multitasking has its positives and is a useful skill to have. However, without a counterbalance of rest and time to take a step back, it can cause you to feel overwhelmed.

So, how do you clear the fog of brain overload? Well, I took some time out and scaled back on activities that could wait (except contractual work, and family responsibilities) to prioritise giving my brain some much-needed rest. Also, during the period when I had brain overload, I refrained from launching new projects and working on my new business. I took a two-month break from podcasting and reduced content creation and embraced quiet time away from social media.

If you are seeking to overcome brain overload, here are some suggestions:

## Disconnect

If you spend excessive time on social media or are glued to your computer screen, it is time to take a break. The constant influx of images, opinions, and noise from technology and social platforms alone can contribute to brain overload. Try to carve out periods in your day where you are not staring at a screen. If you're up for it consider a longer detox. I aim to do at least one-day weekly where I detox from social media.

## Do brain calm activities

Solitude is underrated. Yet the moments you spend alone, free from interruptions and distractions, can be incredibly powerful in combating brain overload. Activities like walking or reading can also bring peace of mind. Aim to spend at least half an hour a day quieting your thoughts.

## Prayer

My morning quiet time daily at 5.30 am with God, reading my bible, reflecting, and praying has been instrumental in managing brain overload. However, when I experience sleep issues, it disrupts my routine, causing me to wake up at 6.30 am. Nevertheless, I am slowly working my way back to be consistent in my morning routine, as I know the many benefits prayer brings peace, clarity, and structure to my day. If you struggle with prayer, ask God for help.

Brain overload is a threat to living exceptional and not expected. How can you process thoughts of change, freedom, or plans to have the courage to act if you are overwhelmed, tired, and unfocused? If you recognise you need a break, take it. Far from hindering or delaying your goals, dreams, or aspirations, diminishing brain overload will empower and replenish you.

*The Lord is my shepherd, I lack nothing. He makes me lie down in green pastures, he leads me beside quiet waters, he refreshes my soul.* **Psalm 23:2-3**

# Challenge Insights

To live an empowered life requires action. However, many people don't take action to explore the possibilities of pursuing a life different from what they have known. So, in September 2023, I created the Living the Empowered Life calendar challenge to empower, inspire, and encourage people on social media to do something new, different, or exciting every day for a month. I also participated in the challenge and gained many insights by engaging in the activities.

The first insight I had was that consistency is crucial in taking part and completing a challenge. Moreover, you have to be intentional in what you set your mind to. Admittedly, on certain days, it felt hard, especially with other life commitments to attend to. However, I pushed through the challenges in a variety of ways. Some days, I combined two daily activities (killing two birds with one stone, so to speak) to complete the challenge. On other days, I did the daily activity early in the day or later in the evening. As they say, it's the taking part that counts, and I took part and gave it my best.

The second insight I gained was that doing a challenge that includes things you love makes it easier. On the days noted to do fun things, I gravitated towards going to free art exhibitions. I enjoyed these activities. Also, it was a great reminder about what living an empowered life is about: doing things that you love, that bring you joy, and doing things you are passionate about.

On one of the day activities, it was about doing something courageous. I am proud that I found the courage to act on something I wanted to do for about a year. I wrote to the Chairwoman of the John Lewis Partnership, Dame Sharon White. She is someone I find inspirational as I read her backstory and listen to quite a few of her interviews on leadership. As someone of the same ethnicity as Sharon, it is encouraging to see her at the top of a recognised organisation. I bought a card and with my nicest fountain pen, wrote an encouraging message to her. Also, I asked if it would be possible to ask her some questions about leadership and possibly get any tips. I took a bus to John Lewis headquarters in Victoria and hand-delivered the card. A week later, I received an email from her PA, thanking me for my kind gesture of sending an encouraging card. I never got to ask her those questions face to face.

I may not have had the expected outcome that I had hoped for, but I did get a result from having the courage to act. The experience taught me that if you don't ask, you don't get. Also, you have to be always willing to do something different from what you have done before. I put off sending her a card for a year. If I knew I would have got a result from finally writing and sending the card, I might have done it sooner.

Overall, I consider the challenge a success. It helped me to understand that challenging myself should be an everyday part of my life. It could be to study a little harder or do one more thing than I am used to and continue to explore where opportunities take me. And that is my encouragement to you challenge yourself to explore life. Do not stay in the box of things that you are used to. When you challenge yourself, you invite growth into your life. Personal insights are the seeds that help you to grow and help you live exceptional and not expected. Never let age or circumstances make you stagnant. Aspire to live an empowered life every single day.

*Brethren, I do not count myself to have apprehended; but one thing I do, forgetting those things which are behind and reaching forward to those things which are ahead, I press toward the goal for the prize of the upward call of God in Christ Jesus.* **Philippians 3:13-14**

# Change Like the Seasons

Just as the year transitions through the seasons of spring, summer, autumn, and winter, we as humans transition through different seasons in our lives, and even though change is a natural part of life many people resist it. Often the resistance stems from a fear of the unknown, the effort and energy required to accommodate change, or a preference for the familiarity of the current situation even if it is unproductive or negative. It's sad the comfort of routine can make even dysfunction feel safe.

In the past, I resisted change because I feared what it would mean for my life. I pondered; would it strip away my sense of self? Would it demand something I couldn't give? Would it feel uncomfortable? The answer turned out to be yes. But that "yes" unfolded gradually as I embarked on the journey of change. As I stopped resisting and embraced the process, the results began to manifest. I grew more confident in making decisions and started seeing life from a fresh perspective. The things I once tolerated or engaged in no longer held space in my life, for their season had passed. It was time to welcome a new chapter. The harsh winter of my life, where I felt stuck and fearful of change, gave way to the promise of spring, a season of transformation and new beginnings. Through my efforts and actions, I moved into the warmth and abundance of summer, where the fruits of change became clear, and in the autumn of life, I took time to reflect with gratitude, appreciating the journey change taught me.

I am deeply grateful for the personal, spiritual, and emotional growth I've experienced through the different seasons of change I've had in my life. It was especially evident in my transition from being an employee to becoming a business owner. Working for various employers for twenty-three years to becoming my own boss, responsible for running a business, was a huge learning curve. It required sacrifices personally and professionally, but every step, even though challenging at times, has been worth it. Embracing different degrees of change in my life powered my transformation. The most important lessons I learned about change are:

## It's Your Choice

Change is an inevitable part of life; nothing stays the same forever. How you respond to change is up to you. You can either welcome it or resist it. To embrace change, I encourage you to keep your heart and mind open and not be rigid with yourself or your life.

## Life Moves in Seasons

Where you are now is not where you will always be. Every season has its purpose, even if it is unclear now. Trust that there is a meaning behind your current phase, even when it's difficult to see.

## Not Everyone Will Support Your Growth

Positive changes in your life are meant for your benefit, not for the approval of others. If you've decided to evolve and grow during this season, stand firm and enjoy the process; it's your journey to embrace.

*While the earth remains, seedtime and harvest, cold and heat, winter and summer, and day and night shall not cease.* **Genesis 8:22**

# Expect the Best Not Less From You

*YEME Empowerment*

# Cut It Off

To cut off what no longer serves you isn't selfish, it's self-care. You deserve peace, joy, and fulfilment in your life. It is a powerful thing when you can release what weighs you down and make space in your life for what you truly desire.

It took me a long time to be brave enough to 'let go and cut off' situations, people, and habits that were holding me back in life. I accommodated too many things that I should have said goodbye to ages ago. For whatever reason, maybe lack of confidence, not wanting to disappoint or hurt others, or simply being used to the familiar, I allowed things to continue, even though I felt weighed down by baggage that wasn't mine to carry. Over time, I realised that feeling overwhelmed and burdened is not the way God wanted me to live. I certainly didn't want to live like this anymore, especially releasing and carrying the weight of the aftermath of childhood sexual abuse for twenty years.

Over the years of cutting off and letting go, I realised it happens in two ways: as a sudden occurrence or a gradual process. Also, some things hurt to cut off while others didn't bother me at all. Here are some things I am still in the process of cutting off:

**Bad habits:** Some have been easy to break, while others have been challenging. For example, I often criticise myself instead of showing myself grace. When I catch myself doing this, I focus on the positives about myself.

**Emotional weight:** This has been closely tied to relationships. I've realised that engaging with certain people comes at the cost of emotional pain. I've started to disconnect and disengage because I am no longer willing to put myself in that position.

**Playing it safe:** I recognise that I shrunk back in doing some things over the years instead of courageously pushing forward. I am gradually cutting off that comfort-zone mindset. I continue to seek opportunities to embrace risk and put myself out there.

The most important question to ask yourself when preparing to cut something out of your life is: **"Is this helping or hindering my growth?"** It's a natural part of life to cut off and let go of what stunts your growth. Even Jesus in the bible emphasised the importance of pruning. So, don't feel guilty for removing toxic things from your life. When you trim away what stunts your growth, you create space to flourish.

*Every branch in Me that does not bear fruit He takes away; and every branch that bears fruit He prunes, that it may bear more fruit.* **John 15:2**

# Discipline is the Key to Success

In whatever you are trying to do, lose weight, build your business, develop new habits, or save money, discipline is the key to success because it will bring order and boundaries to your life and take you to the next level.

I regularly spend time reflecting on my achievements as I sit looking at my vision board in my home office. I have accomplished so much, yet there is so much achieve. When I think about what has made me successful thus far and what will help me to be successful in the future to reach my goals, dreams, and aspirations, discipline is the common theme that weaves itself through my journey. It is one of the key elements that has and will keep me on track to being exceptional and not expected. I must admit I have struggled with discipline. However, I have being making progress in this challenge by praying and asking God for help, reading my bible, and listening to podcasts on the subject. As a result of doing these things, I am already reaping benefits that include a changed mindset that embraces commitment to routine.

Discipline is a mindset habit that must be developed. It involves being intentional in the things you set out to do. Showing up and committing to that thing, whether you feel like it or not. Discipline is not a word that naturally makes people jump for joy because most people associate it with rigid rules. But there is no escaping it. Sooner or later, discipline must come into the equation in all that you do if you want to achieve your goals and dreams.

Medicine tastes unpleasant, but is required to feel better. Certainly, the same applies to discipline. It must be applied to your goal to produce positive results. Here are five tips to help you:

**Set goals**

Goals are an essential part of planning for your life. It is not the number of goals you have; it is about accomplishing the goal you intentionally set. A goal is better than none. Write it down and set manageable steps. Set a time frame for your goal to be completed and try your best to stick to it.

**Have a routine**

Plan your day. Do it the night before if it helps. This will help you to set a routine for discipline. You can also use planning tools such as a diary or wall planner to assist you.

**Just do it**

Do not put off tomorrow what you can do today, because this is where procrastination creeps in. We have all done this at some point in life, but to develop discipline, you must act. Drift is the enemy of discipline.

**Hold yourself accountable**

Conduct daily and weekly check-ins. Have you done what you said you would do? If not, why? Hold yourself accountable. It will help you to keep an eye on yourself. A journal is a good way to keep track of what is and isn't working. Also, it will help you to adjust where necessary.

**Reward yourself**

Make the medicine of discipline easy to swallow by rewarding yourself. No matter how big or small your achievement, acknowledge your progress.

Don't view discipline as rules but as an activity that will streamline your life and enable you to be exceptional and not expected in all you do.

*Now no chastening seems to be joyful for the present, but painful; nevertheless, afterward it yields the peaceable fruit of righteousness to those who have been trained by it.* **Hebrews 12:11**

# Discouragement

I have gone through many periods of discouragement in my life. 2024 was not my best year. At times, I have lacked focus. Discouragement caused me to be inconsistent in doing things that I planned, and it caused me to second-guess myself more than I would like to admit. After much reflection, I identified the root of my discouragement. Unmet and unrealistic expectations, fatigue, and focusing on things outside of my control rather than focusing on what I can do.

As an entrepreneur, I discovered that discouragement is part and parcel of the journey of starting a new business. It is very difficult when you are doing things you have not done before. It can leave you wondering if you are on the right track, especially when you are on such an individual journey. This was my experience, yet it is something most entrepreneurs face. Nevertheless, it affected me deeper than I realised. It is important to recognise the signs of discouragement because it can lead to negative thoughts. After a while, I was able to see work through my discouragement, and it helped me to become more resilient. I want to share with you three things that helped me get my groove back:

## Rest

I am a wife, mother, owner of a business, and founder of a non-profit organisation, amongst other things. I juggle many different tasks and responsibilities, and work long hours, at times, to do it all. It is easy to always be on the go, bouncing from one thing to the next. I discovered this is not a productive thing to do. A change is as good as a rest, as they say. Don't be afraid to say "this can wait" when you feel tired or overwhelmed. It is amazing how rest can refresh your mind. It gives me a different perspective on things and lifts my mood.

## Focus on the positive

What I found helpful when I felt discouraged, was reminiscing on my achievements. Doing this encouraged me to remember all the things I have done so far that, at one point, seemed impossible. This gave me energy to refocus on my long-term vision and goals. Additionally, I made time each day to engage in activities that I enjoy. If you are stuck in the rut of discouragement, find something positive to focus on. Do things that make you feel happy. Do things that encourage you to look forward despite how you feel in this present moment.

**Let go**

One of the biggest contributors to my season of discouragement was focusing on things outside of my control. It is very easy to think that you must be in control of everything when you are responsible for so much. As an entrepreneur, this has been my biggest challenge. It is true that I have a certain responsibility to "make things happen". However, I am only in charge to an extent. Other factors can depend on people and circumstances. I have learned to let go and trust God. The things that are making you discouraged, you must let go of them. You can only do what you can. The rest, I encourage you to pray and trust God to work it out.

There is always something we can learn from our experiences. Recognise this season of discouragement in your life for what it is, part of a process to build you.

*He shall be like a tree planted by the rivers of water, that brings forth its fruit in its season, Whose leaf also shall not wither; And whatever he does shall prosper.* **Psalm 1:3**

# Don't Despise the Day of Small Beginnings

Everyone starts somewhere in life, and usually the starting point is the beginning. Starting something new is often the hardest part as it requires focus and motivation. Furthermore, it requires consistency and energy to keep the momentum going. I can tell you from experience that once the excitement of starting something new settles down, this is where it gets tough to keep going. I remember many years ago—fifteen years ago, in fact, when I released my first book, Daughter Arise, feeling impatient that after two years, I was still doing talks and book signings to small audiences. I can admit that at the time, I felt I should have been hosting bigger events because of all the hard work I had done. Such pride and entitlement. Who was I to feel I deserved more? One evening, as I was getting ready to do a talk and book signing at my daughter's nursery, the Lord God spoke to me and said, 'Never despise the day of small beginnings'. Impacted by those powerful words from that day onwards, I humbled myself and changed my attitude towards small beginnings.

There is nothing wrong with starting small in the things you are trying to do. A lot of people, especially on social media, will only show you when they've achieved their goals and dreams, the moment they have 'arrived'. Rarely do they show you their beginnings, trials, failures, and challenges on their personal journey. What has been sobering for me is that I am still in my small beginning—fourteen years since the book signing at the nursery. I still have not achieved my goals or reached the place I desire to be. Sometimes I get distracted by this fact; however, while waiting, I use the time to pray, acquire further knowledge, invest in self-development, perfect my writing and speaking skills, and continue content creation to build my businesses endeavours. The season of small beginning can last a long time. This is where many people get impatient, lose focus, resent the process, and quit. If you find yourself tempted to give up because you feel you have been stuck in your small beginning for a long time, I encourage you to:

**Be patient**

I have found the key to sticking in the small beginning is to be patient. Nothing happens before its time, and there is a reason you are currently in this stage. Do not try to rush to get ahead. Allow things to unfold in the way they need to.

**Use the time to learn**

Instead of focusing on where you think you should be, use the time to prepare for that moment you hope to one day see. Use your time to hone your craft, practice, and develop the things you need to do. Appreciate what you are learning in this season of your life. Understanding that all that you do in this stage is going to prepare you for what is to come.

## Remain focused

Don't be discouraged in your time of small beginnings. Remain focused on the work you are doing on your goals and dreams. Focus on your achievements so far. Focus on the impact you are having with the things you are doing now. Remember, small beginnings are not forever.

*Do not despise these small beginnings.* **Zechariah 4:10**

## Don't Let People's Opinions of You Become Your Facts

The truth is, people love to give opinions on things they don't know and people they don't know. They see a person on the outside; they do not have a consistent or close relationship with them and may not know them at all, yet they say things about them. For some people, the opinions of others, combined with low self-esteem or confidence, are enough to make that person take on board those opinions as facts about themselves. In doing so, they give the opinionated person influence and control over them.

No one should have that power over you. After all, God is your creator, not people. Do not allow people's opinions of you to become who you believe you are. Note that people who always have opinions about others are never able to reflect and apply change in their own lives. It can make an opinion-driven person mad when they see they don't have influence over the way you see yourself or your life. Good. The only opinion that matters is yours and the Living God.

How YOU see yourself matters. At least good or bad, you can work on the challenges you face. If you don't know how to hold on to the truth about who you are, and struggle with always seeking the opinions of people, hold on to what God says about you. Don't allow people to speak their opinions of you into your life.

*More to be desired are they than gold (word of God), yea, than much fine gold; sweeter also than honey and the honeycomb.* **Psalm 19:10**

# Don't Look Back, Go Forward

It is vital to take forward the lessons of a past year. Not for the purpose of dwelling on the negative, but to reflect. Not to remember the bad, but to focus on the good. The challenges of a past year can serve to elevate a new year.

Of course, there were a few things I was not pleased with in previous years. Certain themes are recurring. I could have managed my personal time better. My focus was a little off, and at times, I prioritised work a bit too much. Some decisions came with a cost, a sacrifice, and most certainly created more work. However, even though I probably could have done things differently, I refuse to have regrets. Instead, I use the lessons of previous years to do better and become better. Yesterday is in the past, and I can only work on making my present decisions count towards a positive and enriched future.

If your past years were not as you had hoped, I encourage you not to dwell on it. Use the perceived shortcomings as fuel for a new year. Put your past mistakes, failures, and disappointments behind you and look for the positives. Don't look back, go forward with the hope that your future will be brighter than you could ever imagine.

*Now the Lord blessed the latter days of Job more than his beginning.* **Job 42:12**

# Do something new

Spring is the perfect time to do something new. What are the things you have always wanted to do but have not done? I encourage you to spring forward and give those things a try. Life is about experiencing life. So, get out of your comfort zone and do something different.

## Cultivate a growth mindset

Some things do take time to bloom, such as a growth mindset. If you have started to plant the seeds (with new knowledge, information, and activity), they will need watering continually. Are you in the process of doing a new thing or making life changes? Continue to strengthen your progress by following up with action steps. Cultivating a growth mindset is about breaking away from any habits, ways, or behaviours holding you back. In due time, you will see the bloom of results.

Spring forward is about putting the former things behind you to anticipate new things, the new changes you want to make in your life. Go forward with bold courage and make room to grow.

*See, I am doing a new thing! Now it springs up; do you not perceive it? I am making a way in the wilderness and streams in the wasteland.* **Isaiah 43:19**

# Even if You Fail Try Again

I don't think anyone in life gets things right the first time they try to do something. Most of the time, getting things right involves a process of failing, learning, experimenting, and experience to enable us to do better next time. Failure is something that people try to avoid. The very thought of it fills people with dread. However, failure is part of the cycle of life. It can happen once, a dozen times, or a hundred times, depending on what each of us is trying to attempt, learn, overcome or achieve. Jesus recognised that as humans, not only do we fail morally in living up to God's standards, but also in our failure towards others. That is why Peter said "Lord, how many times should I forgive my brother who sins against me?", and put a limit of seven times; Jesus said seventy times seven **(Matthew 18:21-35)**.

Imagine having this grace towards our own failings. The truth is, it is easy after the first time let alone the seventh time of failing to give up and not try again. You may say 'How many times do I fail before I get it right? Before I get a breakthrough?', or, 'I can't face the shame of trying again as people have seen me try and fail'. Also, frustration, disappointment, and impatience will demand that you dare not try again. But by the grace of God, as you are still here, you have the opportunity to try and fail again; therefore, you should try. Don't lose hope or give up yet. Here are some tips to help you succeed:

**Ask God for help**

God is an ever-present help in times of trouble. Where we fail in our own strength, we can succeed in His strength, especially if the area of failure involves addiction or ingrained habits. God is gracious and merciful to us and extends grace to us in our failings. You do not need to be perfect or have the right words to talk to God. Ask for help, and God will make a way for you.

**Learn from previous failures**

As I mentioned, failures, mistakes, and errors, allow us the time to learn and the opportunity to do things differently. If you could do that thing again, what would you do differently next time? What is the area or stage you keep failing at? Once you identify your failing, you can specifically look at resources or support to help overcome that area of challenge.

**Adjust your mindset from a defeat stance to a conqueror position**

Repeated failure can easily set your mind in a defeatist position. Even if you fail and fail again, you must tell yourself you can and *will* succeed. Keep your eye on your goal and never give up. As the famous quote states,' If at first you don't succeed, dust yourself off and try again!'.

*And we know that in all things God works for the good of those who love God, to those who are called according to his purpose.* **Romans 8:28**

# Give Freely

Today we live in a society that is selfish, self-centred, and entitled. It seems rare to find people who give, with the hope of anything in return; even to give in the first place. The beauty of giving is a wonderful act. It is an act of kindness that everyone would benefit from doing from time to time.

When I think about the ultimate act of kindness I think about Jesus and his sacrifice. He gave his life on the cross so that mankind could be reconciled with God. He did not come to be served but to serve and gave his life as a ransom for many **(Mark 10:45).** God so loved the world that he gave his one and only son, *that whoever believes in him shall not perish but have eternal life* **(John 3:16).** God gave us a free gift, one that none of us deserve. Imagine giving someone you love very much as a sacrifice for people who don't even recognise or appreciate it. Yet God gave without expectation or conditions.

The truth is, you are more blessed to give than to receive. Especially if you give without reminding the person of what you gave. To remind the person of your generosity towards them invalidates your efforts and shows that your giving never came from a genuine place within your heart or with the right intentions.

If you want to be exceptional and not expected, learn to give without conditions. Furthermore, I challenge you to give not out of surplus in your life, but when it is challenging for you to give. To do this releases a level of freedom in your life because it signifies that your giving is not controlled by your circumstances, but out of the desire to bestow kindness on someone in their time of need.

*Whoever is kind to the poor lends to the Lord, and he will reward them for what they have done.* **Proverbs 19:1**

# Good Conversation

When was the last time you had a good conversation? And no, I'm not talking about gossip. I am talking about a conversation with someone you enjoy talking to which uplifts, empowers, encourages, or has a positive effect on both of you. These conversations for me are few and far between. Life is so busy, and time always seems to be occupied with other things. However, when I get to have a meaningful conversation, it is always a blessing. I was blessed to speak with a friend of mine who I had not spoken to in ages. She is and has always been an encourager. She supports me in the work I do on my nonprofit organisation, as she co-facilitates some of the support group sessions that I organise. This is invaluable to the women who attend the group. She is someone who understands the power and value of uplifting others.

What I enjoy about our relationship is even though we don't speak often, when we do finally catch up, we pick up our conversation where we left it. Our talks are always enriching. There was a point in my life after the pandemic, when I was feeling discouraged, tired, and disillusioned. I talked to this friend, and after our talk, I came away with a feeling of positivity, and motivated to keep going. Have you heard the saying, 'a problem shared is a problem halved'? That is what the power of a good conversation can do; it can share the burden of a problem. Good conversation has many positives. It helps you let out stress. Helps you view things from a different perspective. And when the person you are conversing with has your best interests at heart, they will encourage and pray for you (if they are a person of faith).

It should be noted that there are parameters to a good conversation; basically, an environment where it can thrive. It should be with someone you trust, not with a known gossip, negative, or untrustworthy person. Effective listening, empathy, and knowledge can enrich the conversation. In the confines of this relationship, reciprocity is in the midst. Both individuals give, take, and add value to the experience.

If you are seeking to live an empowered life, conversation should be part of it. Meaning that talking with and being listened to by someone you can talk to about your goals, dreams, hopes and fears, will benefit you on your journey to being exceptional not expected. Of course, the ultimate conversation that will change your life is with Jesus. Invite him into your heart and talk to him about your life plans, and he will lead you into all truth and impart to you the answers you have been searching for. It will be the most important conversation you will have in your life—and the best.

*Behold, I stand at the door and knock. If anyone hears My voice and opens the door, I will come in to him and dine with him, and he with Me.* **Revelation 3:20**

# Holding On to The Past Is Expensive

Many people hold on to past resentment, hurt, unforgiveness, heartbreak, insecurities, trauma, fear, and doubts. The consequence of holding on to the past can include feelings of depression, negativity, stagnation, anger, and trust issues. It is important to realise that holding on to the past is expensive. The cost is always paid in the present or future of the person.

Holding on to the past is like clenching your fists. Because you won't let whatever it is go, you cannot hold anything else. How can you embrace new opportunities when you're still gripping onto things that stunt your growth? If this resonates with you, maybe it's time to let go of what is holding you back so that you can welcome the exciting possibilities life has to offer. Clinging to the past won't shape a better future—trust me, I've been there. I used to struggle with letting go of the hurt others had caused me. It made me grudgeful, resentful, and in the end, the only person I was hurting was myself. But with God's grace, I learned to forgive and release the past.

Holding on to the past only holds you back, keeping you in an unproductive and unhealthy place that prevents you from reaching your full potential. I encourage you today to stop paying the price of living in the past. Wondering how? Here's what you can do:

## Forgive

Forgiveness isn't just a feeling; it's an action. You may not feel ready to forgive, but it's crucial for liberating yourself from the past. When I faced the challenge of forgiving those who caused me significant pain, I realised it was a process I had to revisit repeatedly. Each time the memory of their actions returned, I had to consciously remind myself, that I had already forgiven them. This was no easy task, but it was essential. I also reflected on how Jesus had forgiven me, and I understood that if I wanted to receive forgiveness from God for my own faults, I needed to extend that same grace to others. Also, seeking therapy can be beneficial, especially if you've experienced trauma in your past.

## Consider what you want more

Do you wish to break free from the constant burden of your past, or do you prefer to remain trapped by the pain you've endured? Would you rather embrace peace instead of sadness, anger, or regret? Are you interested in discovering what it truly means to live exceptionally rather than merely as expected, or do you want to be shaped and limited by the experiences that have held you captive for so long? The choice is yours to make. What do you want more? The past, or your future? It may be a challenging journey to address your past, but as you resolve it piece by piece, the hurt, doubt, fear, and pain will lessen.

You deserve better than to be held back by past pain. To stay in that place is expensive. Pay the price and let it go. In doing so, you will open yourself up to a brighter future.

*Let your eyes look straight ahead, and your eyelids look right before you.* **Proverbs 4:2**5

# It Will Be Worth
# It in the End

*YEME Empowerment*

# How to Say Goodbye to a Year

I have realised from keeping journals for over twenty years that sometimes one year is better than another. Nevertheless, whatever the year, I have learned to be thankful. Also, as time has gone by, I have got into the habit of saying goodbye to each year. I think it is important not to let the year pass without acknowledging and recognising it for what it was. I believe it is an essential part of personal development and growth.

Each year has its ups and downs, challenges and achievements, as well as moments of revelation and clarity. I love to read for reflection, my prayer and year journals. I am always surprised by how I overcame challenges, the things I once thought were important that I forgot, and the moments I documented to remember. Many things can happen in a year, so how do you say goodbye? By doing three simple things:

**Reflect on the year**

What has stood out for you? What are you proud of? What do you need to work on? Reflecting on the year will help you gauge where you are and help you take stock of your life.

**Be thankful**

For the good and bad times. It will help you in all aspects of life.

**Look for the positives**

It is easy to remember the negative things that happen in a year. Let us say goodbye to the previous year by focusing on the great and positive things we have achieved. No matter if they are big or small moments. Let them be encouragement for what we hope the upcoming year will be.

*Every good and perfect gift is from above, coming down from the Father of the heavenly lights, who does not change like shifting shadows.* **James 1:17**

# Legacy Over Likes

In this social media age that we live in, the term 'influencer' has good and bad connotations. Influence can be used for good or bad purposes. You have people who use their influence to encourage others to engage in materialism, gluttony (in the form of mukbang), or gossip, which can lead to strife and confusion. And there are influencers who use their platforms to encourage, raise awareness of societal issues, or document a journey of transformation.

One thing is for sure: if you are gifted with the power of influence, whether good or bad, when you pass away, what you promoted will be what you are remembered for. However, this question probably does not come into the equation for people whose motivation is just to be first to share their opinion, but who want to be remembered for the wrong things. A negative legacy is the consequence of sharing without applying wisdom and knowledge.

If you want to leave a positive legacy wherever you have influence, your family, community, business, or social arena, it is wise not to follow the trend of what everyone else is doing but to be led by God. To be exceptional and not expected means that if you are called to be a positive force in the lives of others, you use your life to positively encourage others. It is not the number of followers, views, clicks, and likes that equate to legacy. What contributes to legacy is positive influence, inspiration, impact, helping others, kindness, adding value to others, and authenticity. These are some of the main foundations on which legacy is built.

So, if you are influential, the decision you must make is whether you want the applause and attention of *now* or the impact *later* (which in this life you may only get a glimpse of). Legacy in its entirety is only recognised and understood years, decades, or centuries later. We only have to look at the life of Jesus Christ to understand that. I don't know about you, but I choose legacy because I have seen a snapshot of the lives God has used me to impact in a positive way. If you are a creative person or influencer, don't get caught up in believing that because you are not promoting negative things, or that you may not have views, clicks, and subscribers, you are not doing anything worthwhile. It may not be noticed until after you have left this world, and it's then that your legacy will be remembered. Don't let anything deter you from having a positive impact on those around you.

*Heaven and earth will pass away, but My words will by no means pass away.* **Matthew 24:35**

# Live Empowered

My journey to living an empowered life started at thirty-five years old. It was one of the hardest, most challenging, and rewarding decisions I have made to pursue the life I desired to live. As I have shared throughout my books and social media content, early traumatic life experiences caused significant setbacks in my life. However, I do not look back on this period of my life with regret. Instead, I choose to focus on what I can do in the here and now to fulfil my potential.

One of the most important lessons I learned from things that happened in my life that were outside my control is that I have the power to choose what I can do in the presence of such circumstances. For a long time, I flowed with the narrative of my trauma; that I was helpless—because I had battled depression, low confidence, and self-esteem. That I would in some way, shape, or form be affected for the rest of my life by my past experience. But as I confronted each challenge left in the aftermath of childhood sexual abuse, I found that rather than it being an albatross around my neck, the process of overcoming its obstacles became a source of encouragement and driving factor in my future success.

My past motivated me to live empowered. The version of life I was living up until my early thirties felt hopeless. I had no real vision or purpose; I was just being pushed along with the tide of life until I decided to give a different side of life a try. I discovered that courage is the vehicle that takes you from feeling *disempowered* in life to *empowered*. It takes you from where you are to where you want to be. You must let courage and desire for change guide you towards the life you want, especially when other people put expectations and demands on how they believe you should live your life. It is a natural assumption for people to believe that a lack of money stops you from living empowered. Of course, having money is beneficial in life as it eases financial stress and may bring a sense of freedom. But you don't need to have money first to live empowered. What you need is a made-up mind and the courage to act—these two things can open more doors than you ever imagined. It takes real bravery to pursue the life you want, to live a life unique to God's will for you, and pursue your dreams later in life, especially when society tends to think dreams are for the pursuit of the young. Choosing this path on the cusp of midlife, like I did at thirty-five years old or older, is not silly or irresponsible. It's courageous to know that despite the challenges, fear, and doubts, you still move forward, forging life in the way you want.

So, as someone living empowered, I encourage you to live empowered and with purpose. Seek new experiences, create new memories, live life for you, and follow your dreams. After all, God has gifted you with life and wants you to live it with purpose, not restricted by circumstances that are not aligned with His plan for you. Your family, friends, or even (if you have them) your children cannot live the life you want for yourself. Dance to the life rhythm God has instilled inside, free from the orchestra of others' opinions.

*Blessed is she who believed, for there will be a fulfilment of those things which were told her from the Lord."* **Luke 1:45**

# Not Done Before Does Not Mean Impossible

For all you visionaries, creatives, entrepreneurs, idea-ists (I know that's not a real word!), and those of you with a dream to do something new, different, or out of the box, don't worry if people don't get what you are trying to do. You cannot expect people to conceive the vision you are trying to bring forth. Don't let people's lack of enthusiasm, doubts, or misunderstanding discourage you. Don't take it as a sign that what you are attempting to do is impossible, especially if it has not been done before. Keep focused, get inspiration, and keep motivated.

It is a lonely journey when you are attempting to do something that has not been done before or done in a way that you are attempting to do. I have experienced this challenge in many things the Lord has called me to do. That's why I wrote about my experiences in my third book, *Into the Unknown*. You must see your ideas through to the end. If you are feeling tempted to give up, here are three tips from my book Into the Unknown to encourage you:

## Seize the day

There is never going to be a perfect time to take a chance and attempt the so-called impossible.

Circumstances will never be perfect. The timing may not necessarily be right either. Seize the day. Don't wait. The outcome may surprise you in a way you did not expect.

## Just because it is difficult does not mean it is not right

If things are difficult for you on your journey of attempting the perceived impossible, do not automatically think you are on the wrong path. Let God be your guide, not your feelings or people.

## Be your biggest cheerleader

When no one else is cheering you on or supporting you, you will have to find a way to encourage yourself. Allow your inspiration to be your encouragement. Also, use other things to be your cheerleader—podcasts, books, encouragement from others who have done or attempted to do what you are trying to do.

Remember, the best innovations and ideas are never understood in the moment. The dream you are chasing won't be understood by those who don't have dreams. So, drown out the unnecessary noise—and go for it!

*Is anything too hard for the Lord?* **Genesis 18:14**

# Not Everyone Can Be Trusted With Your Pearls

Sometimes when we lack discernment and wisdom, we give our best and our trust to people who don't deserve it. We make the mistake because we never tested them to find out if they could be trusted with our most precious asset: our heart. I had to learn the hard way many times, especially in my teenage years, twenties, and early thirties, the truth about people. You see, I was always a person who wore my heart on my sleeve. If I was feeling hurt or upset, it was natural for me to speak to someone I knew to get advice about what was troubling me. I thought during those times in my life, the people I had around me at the time cared for me, but what I came to find out in the most brutal and humiliating way is that they cared nothing for me. Instead, these individuals only had a listening ear because they wanted to weaponise my most vulnerable moments against me to try and destroy me. These experiences sobered me with wisdom and helped me to understand to be careful who I share the vulnerable things of my heart with.

Part of the Exceptional Not Expected life ethos includes assessing the quality of our relationships. Because relationships are an important part of life, we need to consider who we share our heart matters with. More importantly, whether those people are trustworthy and reliable. You see, when these elements are present, besides reciprocal care, love, and respect, it is the foundation for building a trusting relationship. This indicates that the matters of the heart that you both share are cherished with care.

Some of you have lost your faith in relationships. Some of you have been left broken-hearted by relationships. Some of you, for this very reason, don't have relationships because you gave your 'pearls' (your heart and the things pertaining to it) to swine (uncaring, scrupulous people). That is why Jesus said, *'Don't throw your pearls to swine'*. Giving your best to people who do not care for what you give, who do not care for your heart, will result in them mistreating, misusing, and abusing you. They think nothing of trashing the trust you give them. But hopefully, like me, you have learned from your experience and become more discerning. My hope for you is that even though you feel you can never share your heart (pearl) again, you *will* be able to do so again, with wisdom, knowledge, and understanding of who you share with.

We are made to be in a relationship. The most important relationship is first with our creator, the Living God, and then with other people. Relationships are cultivated through trial and error.

However, we cannot be reckless with our pearl. We must be wise in who we confide and trust in, whether in friendships or relationships, and who better to guide us than the Lord God. Your heart is your most valuable asset—don't be reckless with it.

*Do not throw your pearl to swine lest they trample them under their feet and turn and tear you to pieces.* **Matthew 7:6**

# One Step Back in Order
# To Step Forward

Sometimes in life, you must take one step back to go forward. This shouldn't be viewed as a negative thing because in the long run, it will put you in the place you need to be.

I used to have a mindset that viewed any step back as a negative thing; I often viewed it as a setback. However, as I've matured, reflected on my life experiences, encountered challenges as an entrepreneur, read books by successful people, and had conversations with people who had to take a step back in life for many reasons, I've come to understand that taking a step back is a positive thing in certain circumstances. For example, women entrepreneurs who have a business. Some face a shortage of financial capital to invest in their business. Rather than get a bank loan or apply for credit, they re-enter the world of traditional employment for a set period. This may be perceived as a step back, but it is a step forward because it is allowing them to get the capital needed to advance their business. On the other hand, if you are taking a step back into relationships or situations that are harmful to you, this is not a good step back. A good step back is one that is preparing, helping, or assisting you positively in the things of your future.

So, if your one step back is contributing to advancing your future, consider the benefits. It allows you to reevaluate the next steps to your goals; allows you time to acquire extra knowledge, skills, and resources, and strengthens your future.

If you must take a step back don't be discouraged. Use it to your advantage. Everything happens for a reason.

*Commit your works to the Lord, and your thoughts will be established.* **Proverbs 16:3**

# Opportunity Knocks

Many people believe that opportunities are handed to them. Sometimes this is true. However, the majority of the time, you have to create the opportunities you want. That is how I got to where I am today.

I was reminded of the power of opportunities when I interviewed Counsellor Kemi Akinola (episode fifty-eight of Living the Empowered Life Podcast). Her story is an example of what happens when you open yourself up to the possibilities that opportunities can bring. She is the Deputy Leader of Wandsworth Council and is a history-maker. She is the first woman in this position in the Labour Party's 119-year history and the first black woman to hold this position. This achievement is something to acknowledge and celebrate, and there are some important lessons about opportunity from her story that I want to share with you.

### Even when life feels like it has stopped keep moving

Seventeen years ago, Kemi was involved in a road accident. She was knocked off her bike. This resulted in her being in a coma for two months. Consequently, she was left with a brain injury. For a period, Kemi could not work, yet that did not stop her. A year into her healing journey, driven by boredom and wanting to keep busy, she started volunteering with an organisation. Six years later, she started her own charitable organisation to support those affected by food poverty. She didn't let the fact that she could not do certain things, stop her from looking for new opportunities to do things she hadn't done before.

Life has a way of taking us on detours. However, we can still find opportunities along the way. Those moments in life we think are a dead end are a door to a new beginning.

## Self-belief is a must

When Kemi decided to run in her local constituency for the position of Councillor, she said self-belief was a driving factor. She had never been in politics before; she was entering into new territory. Nevertheless, she believed in herself, her ability, her experiences, and her capabilities. Moreover, she had a vision and purpose.

If you want to live an empowered life and be exceptional and not expected, you must develop self-belief. You must believe you can achieve your goals and dreams, even if your current reality, people, and circumstances tell you differently. You must decide that you will achieve whatever it is that you want. It may take months, years, or decades. Consequently, you might experience disappointment, setbacks, or failure along the way. However, if you have self-belief and determination, you will be successful in the end. Never give in.

## Do what others won't do

Hard work, more responsibility, and personal sacrifice of time had put other people off the opportunity to apply for the leadership position. However, it did not deter Councillor Kemi from putting herself forward. Driven by her vision and motivation to help the underdog, she decided to seize the opportunity to make a difference.

The thing you need to know about an opportunity is that it involves doing the hard things. Furthermore, it involves changing your mindset to understand that opportunity often demands doing things outside your comfort zone.

To be willing to do what others won't do (without morally compromising yourself) takes courage and dedication. Where others moan and complain about the hard work required, a person who understands the value of opportunities will think of the benefits it will bring in the long term, whilst going through the challenges in the short term. Furthermore, they will be willing to develop themselves in the midst of the opportunity.

If you want to create or take opportunities, remember it is your decision on where you allow it to take you and define you. Opportunities are everywhere if you allow yourself to see them. All you need to pursue them is self-belief, courage, and a purpose, and the rest will follow.

*If they had been thinking of the country they had left, they would have had opportunity to return.* **Hebrews 11:15**

# Rejection Sensitivity

Throughout my podcast episodes (you'll find details about the podcast at the end of the book), I have talked about courage, risk, purpose, personal identity, and many other essential aspects of living an empowered life. As I was reviewing the episode index, I realised there was one important topic I hadn't addressed yet—rejection.

Rejection is often seen by many people as one of life's 'icks' (refer to the "You Can't Avoid the Icks of Life" book entry). Rejection is something nobody enjoys, and most would avoid it if they could. The sting of rejection can lead to feelings of pain, insecurity, embarrassment, humiliation, fear, and sometimes even depression. It can show up in many forms—whether from another person, a life experience, a decision you've made, or even in the pursuit of your goal or dream. Sometimes, even telling the truth can cause rejection if it's not well received.

Do you know there is a condition called rejection-sensitive dysphoria. It occurs when a person feels intense emotional pain related to rejection. The word "dysphoria" comes from an ancient Greek word that describes a strong—if not overwhelming—feeling of pain or discomfort. Signs of Rejection Sensitive

Dysphoria include being easily embarrassed or ashamed. having an emotional outburst and getting angry when rejected. For some people, the fear of rejection runs deep, and that can be for several reasons: setting impossibly high standards, experiencing low self-esteem, feeling anxious, especially in social settings, and having issues with relationships.

I've faced rejection many times in my life. In my third book, Into the Unknown, I share several personal experiences of rejection: being rejected by my birth family, applying for jobs, and in relationships. People have rejected what I was doing and the changes they saw in me. Perhaps the most difficult rejection I have faced is in business because I openly professed my faith in Jesus Christ. I won't lie—it's tough to acknowledge that had I not credited Jesus and given God the glory for my life transformation and the success I enjoy today, I might have been easily accepted and further ahead in business. But I have no regrets. The experience, though painful, has toughened my skin, so to speak, and has been a sobering reminder as a Christian that professing my faith will come with a cost.

Despite facing rejection, I have found a way to turn it into a source of empowerment. Each rejection has become a teaching moment: an opportunity for self-reflection, growth, and learning. I have used these experiences to build resilience and character, examining whether there is any truth in the feedback I received. Ultimately, rejection helped me endure life's challenges with greater strength.

In today's social media era and the culture that revolves around seeking likes and validation, rejection is often viewed negatively. Many individuals strive for approval, love, and recognition through these social apps. However, this culture has not equipped people to anticipate, manage, or accept rejection and has negated an important part of the lessons that shape life. Rejection is commonly perceived negatively, however, some of history's most notable figures are remembered for their experiences of rejection. A prominent example is Jesus Christ, who faced rejection for boldly declaring his identity as the Son of God. Even now, his message of the Gospel is rejected by many. Nevertheless, Jesus exemplified the ultimate act of love for those who despised him by sacrificing himself on the cross, allowing us to be reconciled with God **(John 3:16).**

Truthfully, I can tell you from my personal knowledge and varied life experiences that rejection is part of life. Not everyone is going to accept you, like you, or your choices and decisions. There may be times in life when people tell you the truth about something that you've done or about a choice or decision you've made, and you will be rejected for it. If you are daring to live exceptional and not expected, or seeking to live an empowered life, there is a strong possibility you will experience rejection. Simply choosing another path in life different from what those around you expect, can cause you to be rejected. Also, rejection can come in the form of rejection of your ideas, rejection of you pursuing a new thing, or rejection of the positive changes you've made as a person.

You need to decide how to respond to real and perceived rejection. You can either let it pull you into a downward spiral or harness it as a source of empowerment. Here are some tips for dealing with rejection:

## Don't turn it inwards, and don't take it personally

Rejection is one of those experiences that can make you question everything about yourself. A single negative comment can lead you down a destructive path if you let it. Whether it's people not engaging with you or facing repeated job rejections, it's easy to let rejection make you feel discouraged. It's important not to internalise these feelings.

## Try to accept rejection in a positive way

It might sound strange, but what if that rejection was God's way of protecting you? This is a common saying among Christians. Consider this: you can't truly know people's intentions or predict the outcomes of your decisions or opportunities that appear ideal. Only God has a complete view of everything. So, try to see rejection as a potential blessing, as it could mean that thing wasn't right for you.

Rejection is just as integral to life as success, happiness, and achievement. We need to learn to accept both the good and the bad, the rough and the smooth, as well as acceptance about rejection. Despite certain societal efforts to eliminate rejection and present life as entirely pleasant, it remains a reality we cannot escape. While it may be uncomfortable, recognise that rejection could be preparing you for what lies ahead.

*Open rebuke is better than love carefully concealed.*
**Proverbs 27:5-6**

# Reject Boxes, Labels, and Baggage

Have you ever been boxed in by a job title or labelled because of your background, an experience you have been through, or because of the way you look?

Throughout my life, I have been put in many boxes and labelled many things. When I went through childhood sexual abuse, I was labelled a victim and survivor. When I was taken into government care at thirteen years old, I was called a care kid, and even more crudely, by some, a bin bag kid (a term given to kids in care because when we were moved to different placements, our belongings would be put in a black bin bag).

For over twenty years, I suffered from depression. During that challenging time in my life, assumptions were made about me because I struggled with my mental health. I was labelled "fragile, weak, and incapable" by people who saw my challenges as an infirmity. Furthermore, in particular job roles, my job title became a barrier to opportunities because people defined me by it. And let me not forget, as a black woman, the labels associated with my skin colour and the negative connotations that come with it.

One of the main things I learned from my experience with boxes and labels is that it comes with baggage.

The baggage of other people's expectations based on what they believe you can do, your experience, and how you look. Consequently, the danger of being placed in boxes— whether by other people or by life—or being given labels is that, if you allow them to stick, they expect you to carry their negativity, low expectations, limited vision, leaving you hemmed in, restricted, and stuck. Carrying that baggage will leave you with little energy and motivation to succeed, resulting in damage to your personal development and growth. You deserve more than that. **So, if you are someone weighed down by the boxes, labels, and baggage others have defined you by, I encourage you to:**

### Get to know who you are

Not who others say you are, or your past experiences, or your job title presume you are. Get to know your strengths, your likes, and your dislikes. Engage in things that you like to do. Spend time discovering yourself and avoid negative self-talk and self-limiting beliefs. Mute the voices around you that try to put you in a box with a label.

### Don't live up to other's expectations

In doing so, it puts you in danger of being put in their box, and with that experience comes limitations and estimations based on their assessment of you. If you can set your own expectations, you can adjust them based on your capabilities, experience, and life journey. You can define your life based on things that involve you.

## Find your purpose

More often than not, the intrusiveness of boxes, labels, and baggage arises not only from different life influences, self-issues, and others' expectations but also from not having a sense of purpose and vision for your life. To break out of the confines of boxes and labels, you must not only know who you are but also know your purpose so that when anything tries to impose itself on you, it will be easy to reject. Life purpose gives you vision, focus, direction, a sense of value, and motivation.

To live an empowered life and to be exceptional and not expected requires that you have the courage to reject boxes, labels, and baggage. You know the REAL truth about you that no one else sees. And don't worry about the opinions of others. People have always had low expectations of me, but I KNOW the truth about me and that I am capable of even more than I have achieved so far. I believe in me, and I encourage you to believe in you! You can do more than you know. Reject labels, boxes and baggage that life and others try to impose on you.

*Now to him who is able to do immeasurably more than all we ask or imagine, according to his power that is at work within us.* **Ephesians 3:20**

# Rich Life

I live a rich life. I live a fulfilling and abundant life. I am not rich in money, but I am rich in the things money cannot buy. My life is rich because I intentionally seek to share what I have. I live a rich life because I seek to live my life to the fullest, doing new things, acting on opportunities, developing and using the skills and talents the Lord God has blessed me with. I recognise it takes energy, motivation, and willingness to live a rich life, but in my experience, it is the best way to live.

A rich life is an exceptional and not expected way to live, as many don't want this life. Some ways I exemplify living a rich life are that I draw from my past challenges and hardships to inspire, teach, and empower others. I dedicate my time and money to volunteering and supporting others through Daughter Arise, a non-profit organisation I founded in 2011. I actively look for opportunities to make a difference—whether by giving up my seat on the bus or offering an encouraging word to someone in need. I aim to add value wherever I go, sharing wisdom, encouragement, and knowledge with those around me.

I strive to embody the spirit of abundance, which is the ethos of a rich life. I believe as long as I maintain a heart and mindset to bless others, God will ensure my resources and capacity to give remain limitless. Someone who lives a rich life understands that the positive activity of their life overflows into the lives of others and is influential. You can start to live a rich life today by:

## Adding value wherever you go

Be a help, not a hindrance. Look to add positive value to people and situations that you come across. Have you heard the saying: 'be a blessing wherever you go'? Wherever you and your presence reside, it should be a contribution of positivity.

## Turn your negatives into positives

I have learned from experience that the negative situations that we encounter in life often are at our own detriment for the betterment of others. It takes courage to let go of painful situations and instead use them as teaching moments of wisdom for others. To do so is to turn a negative into a positive. It shows that instead of allowing the disappointments you have experienced to turn you bitter, you have allowed them to do better for someone else.

## Make self-growth and personal development a priority

To live a rich life involves investing in yourself. Partake in activities that develop you. No one knows all in life, and no one is perfect, therefore all we can do is improve, grow, and do better. When we do this, it gives us insight, knowledge, inner standing, and wisdom. How can our life not be enriched when we positively pour into ourselves?

Being rich is deeper than what you earn or materially possess. It is about the quality of your soul, the abundance of your heart, what you do with what you personally have, using what is in your heart and hand to add value and enrich others. Today, I encourage you to be rich!

*Give, and it will be given to you: good measure, pressed down, shaken together, and running over will be put into your bosom. For with the same measure that you use, it will be measured back to you.* **Luke 6:38**

# Self-Love Is the Best Love

I have been single at different times in my adult life, and for the last twenty-two years, I have been in a relationship; married for twenty of those years. However, one thing I have discovered to be true, whether as a single woman or a wife, is that self-love is the best love. When you love yourself, it will hold you steady regardless of whether someone loves you or not. Moreover, it will hold you in times when you may not feel loved in a relationship. When you practice self-love, it will encourage you to treat yourself well no matter the circumstances.

In my earlier years, I defined my love of self on how I was treated in a relationship or by other people. Looking back from a place where I now have good self-esteem and sense of self-worth, I realise my past value system stemmed from my experience of childhood sexual abuse. This experience devalued me in so many ways and left me with a low view of self. It is horrible to be in an emotional state where you depend on another person to validate you through their idea of love. Now, as an older woman who has experienced the love of Jesus and grown in wisdom and knowledge, I no longer seek the love of others to make me feel good inside. Self-love is not dependent on the actions or feelings of others. It is dependent on *you*. Because you have to learn to love yourself. That can be hard if you have not known or been taught *how* to love you. You can start by liking you and accepting that regardless of your struggles, they don't determine whether you deserve love. You can start your journey of self-love by:

## Acknowledging the good things about you

Spend some quiet time thinking about the positive things that make you who you are. For example, if you know that you're kind, thoughtful, forgiving, or creative, write it down. List as many positive qualities as you can, and then reflect on what you have written in the times when you feel bad about yourself.

## Develop and maintain a self-love lifestyle

To learn to develop a self-love routine and lifestyle means knowing what you will respond to. What are the things that make you happy? What things make you feel good about being you? This may take some time to discover, and the starting point could be with what things you wanted to do for yourself, like treating yourself to a style overhaul or a spa day. Therapy could be part of developing a self-care lifestyle if you have recognised that past events in your life have contributed to your lack of self-love. In taking time out each day or on a set day signifies that you take the maintenance of yourself seriously. Make it a daily habit.

## Be at peace with who you are now

Don't deny yourself love because of frustration and disappointment with who you are in life right now. Don't punish yourself for your shortcomings. The best thing you can do is accept who you are now and where you are in life at this moment, and be at peace. Peace allows you the room to nurture yourself with its ambience of patience: it will bring many benefits to your life. The most valuable person to you is you. Learn to appreciate and love yourself. Treat yourself with care, love, and respect. You deserve it.

*The Lord appeared of old to me, saying yes, I have loved you with an everlasting love; Therefore, with loving kindness I have drawn you.* **Jeremiah 3:13**

# Smell the Flowers

Every year, on the King's Road in Chelsea, to coincide with the Chelsea Flower Show, the street is lined with flower displays. I always enjoy the beautiful flower presentation. Moreover, I have wanted to go to the actual show. However, at £120.00 a ticket, it is out of my budget.

Nevertheless, I am grateful to be able to visit this free flower exhibition every year. The level of creativity is awesome. As I stroll in the lovely warm and sunny weather, I gain a new appreciation for the small things in life. For instance, the fact that I have lived to see another day, the gift of creativity, and the ability to walk for many hours. Also, an appreciation that my little outing doesn't cost me a penny (well, almost apart from money spent on my bus fare, a decaff Americano, and a slice of carrot cake!).

I believe an appreciation for the things deemed small in life is crucial to living an empowered life and essential on the journey of being exceptional not expected. Because if you can't appreciate the so-called little things, how will you recognise and appreciate the major things that add value to and enrich your life? The process of 'smelling the flowers' involves reflection, gratitude, contentment, and looking for the blessings in what you already have. I admit that as I have gotten older, it has become more of a reality for me. I have learned— through painful life lessons— that it is not the acquisition of things that makes you happy; it is creating memories, appreciating personal victories, living freely, engaging in life, and discovering what makes you happy. It is so easy in the first-world society that we live in to overlook simplicity, the beauty of nature, the gift of life, and the power of creativity and resourcefulness. The temptation for more is always lurking. However, the things that matter cost you nothing. I've discovered that life is what you make it.

There is no getting away from it; life is tough for many people now. The cost of living is at an all-time high, and there are rumours of a pending recession. People are struggling with mental health and other challenging issues. At times, it is easy when you look at the state of the world to overlook the blessings we already have and be discouraged. Nonetheless, it is important not to focus on the negative things; otherwise, we will become discouraged.

So, I encourage you to appreciate life. Stop and smell the flowers. Appreciate the positive changes you have made. Take pictures and make memories. Find pockets of joy where you can. After all, the things deemed small are often the biggest and most important things we will encounter in life.

*Give thanks in all circumstances; for this is God's will for you in Christ Jesus.* **1 Thessalonians 5:18**

# Spring Forward

Spring is a season for new beginnings. A time to embrace the things that you have spent the previous season preparing for. It is a time to bloom and grow. A time of promise for new things. Winter ways are no longer needed; it is time to spring forward.

However, it can be hard to transition from one season to the next. For instance, the in-between clothes may still be relevant if the weather is unpredictable. Similarly, transitioning your mindset from comfort to a new level of activity can be challenging because of the uncertainty this effort will bring. Nevertheless, even if the transition into a new season is difficult, it is necessary to activate change. With that in mind, if you struggle with life transitions, I want to share three tips to help you spring forward.

## Renew and revitalise

In episode sixty-one of Living the Empowered Life podcast titled: 'spring clean your life', I shared four overlooked areas in life that may need an overhaul: relationships, health, career, and goals. Just like we pay focused attention to spring cleaning our house and de-cluttering things we don't want or need, aspects of our life also need this attention. The spring season is the perfect time to remove from your life those dead things, the barren things, and the things you have outgrown. It is a time to renew and revitalise any area of your life that needs reinvigorating. Moreover, it is a time to reflect and refocus on the goals that you have set at the beginning of the year. I encourage you to make some time to think about the things in your life that need an overhaul.

*See, I am doing a new thing! Now it springs up; do you not perceive it? I am making a way in the wilderness and streams in the wasteland.* **Isaiah 43:19**

# Stop Looking at Yourself in the Here and Now

Can you imagine yourself in the future? Can you imagine yourself doing all the things you thought were impossible, living the dream you believed was unobtainable?

Maybe you can't see it because something is stopping you; looking at yourself in the here and now. I want to encourage you to stop looking at your insecurities, fears, problems, and challenges. Take your eyes off what you currently see and focus your mind and eyes on future possibilities. Take your eyes off where you are and take a step towards your goals. I know it is a big ask, and you may feel it is impossible to do. But if you continue to look at yourself in the here and now, it will leave you stuck and discouraged. It will leave you feeling negative and hopeless.

To have a different view of you and your life, it starts in your mind. It involves imagining possibilities and making choices that align with them. You need to take your mind from expected to exceptional thinking. In cultivating a mindset that promotes future limitless thinking about you and your life, it will impact and influence what you do. You will start to do things you once thought impossible to do; the shackles you have bound yourself in will be broken free.

But only you can break free with your decision to stop looking at yourself in the here and now. It involves using your imagination, having faith, personal vision, fostering future thinking, purpose, and hope. Remember, you are more than your current circumstances, feelings, and experiences. You and your future are a great story waiting to unfold.

*But as it is written: "Eye has not seen, nor ear heard, nor have entered into the heart of man the things which God has prepared for those who love Him."* **1 Corinthians 2:9**

# Taking Risks Is the Bridge You Need To Cross To Make Your Dreams a Reality

*YEME Empowerment*

# Take Care

Do you take care of self-care? Perhaps you think self-care is a time-permitted luxury that you cannot afford. However, without it, it is challenging to live exceptional and not expected. Because taking care of yourself mentally, emotionally, physically, and spiritually will help you to maximise your life.

It is noted in various health and well-being publications that there are seven pillars of self-care: mental, emotional, physical, environmental, spiritual, recreational, and social. In each of these areas, we should invest so that when times of tiredness, burnout, fatigue, or stress come, we can draw from them to replenish and revitalise.

It is far too easy to treat self-care as an afterthought. As women, we are used to juggling several things at once, firing on all cylinders, morning to night. Besides being a wife and mother, as an entrepreneur, wearing many hats is often a requirement that comes with the territory. However, I found being in this mode of ultra-busyness counterproductive, because how can I achieve all my goals and be at my best when I'm tired and unfocused? Something has to give. I decided to change how I do things. I listen to my body and rest when I need to, spend time with

God daily, and of course, have my cake and coffee. I also take Friday mornings off, and my creative Friday afternoons are mandatory. I am now in year seven of running a business; it was time to switch things up.

On episode sixty-six of my podcast, Living the Empowered Life , my guest, Niki, talked about her journey from burnout to self-care. It was an insightful interview, and her story about how burnout affected her physical health was a cautionary tale about what can possibly happen when we decide to push through work without regular breaks. However, in her journey through these challenges, Niki discovered a less stressful and meaningful career as a self-care coach. She is a remarkable woman and a great example of someone who takes self-care seriously. One of the biggest takeaways from the interview that I will remember is not to feel guilty if I need to take extra breaks or an afternoon nap. Self-care is taking care of myself, and it should be a priority.

Today, I encourage you to think about what you can do to enhance your self-care. You can start with small things, and when the time is right, progress to bigger or different things. The most important thing is to start to taking care of yourself. After all, don't you want to be the best version of yourself so that you can live the life that you have always wanted?

*Come unto me, all ye that labour and are heavy laden, and I will give you rest.* **Matthew 11:28**

# The Best Relationship

2024 was the year I gained significant insight into relationships. This topic was not a planned focus, but reading the book Covenant Relationships by Keith Intrater prompted me to reflect on how my relationship with God, myself, and others can either enhance or hinder my journey to living exceptional and not expected.

My most important relationship is with God. This relationship provides direction, a solid foundation, peace, and security. Through it, I can be honest and open with God about my insecurities, fears, hopes, and dreams. Guided by God's wisdom, I can become the woman I want to be, aligning my life with His will, vision, and purpose. Moreover, God equips me to face any circumstances that come my way. The empowerment God gives inspires me to live my life uniquely, which offers true freedom. This relationship profoundly influences how I relate to myself and others.

These revelations gave me further fruit for thought after my interview with author and marriage coach Samantha Kaaua, about her book, *"Finding Beauty in Your Broken Pieces: The Art and Science of Transforming Any Relationship."* This insightful book explores the complexities of intimate connections and provides a roadmap for overcoming challenges in relationships to emerge stronger and fulfilled. Our discussion gave me a lot to ponder. I realised that no one teaches us how to be in a relationship, even with ourselves. Often, our parents' relationships with each other serve as our first example. Nevertheless, whether these examples are positive or negative, subconsciously, I believe we carry them into our significant relationships throughout life. Beyond these early lessons, we often learn about relationships through trial and error unless we seek out understanding or guidance from people with expertise in this area. I found Samantha to be a good person to turn to for advice and guidance on this subject.

Samantha emphasised the importance of getting to know and love yourself, first. In doing so, this self-awareness and self-love will build your inner strength and help you stay grounded during challenging times in any relationship. Having a relationship with yourself is essential for leading an empowered life. It fosters self-awareness, self-acceptance, and self-love, all of which contribute to personal empowerment and positive relationships. It also:

## Improves Decision-Making

Knowing yourself helps clarify your values and life goals, guiding you to make decisions aligned with your true desires and long-term happiness.

## Enhanced Relationships

Self-awareness and acceptance improve your communication skills, as you are more in tune with your needs and can express them clearly to others.

## Mutual Respect

When you respect and value yourself, you set a standard for how others should treat you, fostering healthier and more respectful relationships.

Relationships are an integral part of life. The key to understanding relationships lies in the foundation upon which you learn about them, as this influences every relationship you have. However, the most crucial relationships are with God and yourself. If you invest in these two areas, your life will be enriched and grounded. Furthermore, you'll have a solid foundation to steady you in times of external relationship struggles. You deserve to have the best relationship with yourself and with others.

*Though one may be overpowered by another, two can withstand him. And a threefold cord is not quickly broken.* **Ecclesiastes 4:12**

# The Easiest Thing Is Often
# the Hardest Thing to Do

Why is deciding and taking action to go after your dreams, or to do something new or different, or make life changes difficult? Why does the thing that seems so easy often seem the hardest thing to do? I am not sure what most people would say when asked this question, but I know from personal experience that it possibly has something to do with the prospect that change, sacrifice, leaving the comfort zone, or upsetting other people could be involved.

You know why it's hard for you to do what you want to do. You know what you need to do, yet you don't do it. You know what you are currently doing or the way you are living is not making you happy or bringing you peace, yet you can't commit to a decision to try something else.

Believe me, I understand your dilemma. As I mentioned in my book *Into the Unknown, a Journey of Faith, Risk, and Courage*, when I decided to leave traditional employment to start my own business, I spent many nights wrangling about whether to do it or not. And the funny thing is, all the things that kept me in an indecisive state (will I be able to pay my bills, how will I still contribute to my family, where will I find business) had nothing to do with the decision I finally made to take the plunge; it was everything to do with not being happy just surviving in another toxic workplace when I could try my dream of starting my own empowerment company. The internal wrestling lasted eighteen months before I decided to act.

And that is what it comes down to. The desire to pursue a dream longing in your heart outweighs the other things that stand in the way. It's the desire that encourages the willingness to take a risk and figure it out as you go along. It is the desire for life change that makes it easy to do the thing that is assumed to be hard to do. And what you need to understand is that it is totally normal to perceive something as hard if you have never tried or attempted your goal or dream before; it is not the reason you should not try.

Taking the first step is hard to do. However, the best way to do the hard thing is to do it. Once you get over that initial fear and get going by taking the first step you can always reflect and reassess what you need to do. Know that it will be hard, but keep in mind why you made the decision in the first place to do the hard thing. Once you take that first step, you'll realise it was easy to start and wonder why you didn't do it sooner.

*My brethren, count it all joy when you fall into various trials.* **James 1:2**

# The Promise of a Breakthrough

Engaging in master's degree study over the past couple of years has proven to be one of the best self-development tools I've experienced on my journey to being exceptional not expected. Throughout this invaluable journey, I've honed my critical thinking skills, expanded my vocabulary, cultivated curiosity, and enhanced my research and investigative skills. Most significantly, tackling my dissertation taught me a profound lesson when I faced the brink of quitting. I confronted a pivotal choice: succumb to breakdown or push through to a breakthrough.

It's surreal to think about how I nearly quit at the most crucial point of my study because I felt sure I would fail. When I received the results of my dissertation mark, I was genuinely surprised to see that I passed. The last module was extremely challenging. I'll admit I didn't enjoy it. Nevertheless, despite those feelings, I persevered to the end. I had to dig deep and find different tools and resources to help me progress: YouTube videos, downloadable templates, books, coaching sessions, and conversations with the supervisor and tutor. At times, I felt it was an impossible task to finish. But I kept chipping away at my dissertation bit by bit, and in the end, I experienced a breakthrough.

You see, what I learned about breakthroughs, is that they are a gradual process of consistent action rather than abrupt leaps to the next or final stage. Sometimes, when we look for that suddenness of big progress, we can miss the seemingly small, significant steps of progression. I learned that breakthroughs come gradually. And when they happen, it is always a surprising and welcome moment. If you are doing hard things and you are on the verge of giving up, I encourage you to:

## Find help

What do you need to help you get to the next step? Is it support? Is it information? Whatever you need, first try to find it through avenues you already have to hand. For example, help from your network. Is there anyone who has done the things you are attempting to do? If so, this is a fantastic source of insight and knowledge. YouTube is also a great free medium with a wealth of knowledge on how to do most things.

## Be repetitive

The breakthrough comes in persistent, consistent steps. While it is not fun, you will see results in the things you are trying to get a breakthrough in. Be repetitive and keep focused!

## Keep your eye on the prize

What makes the hard work of a breakthrough worth it? The prize, of course! Keep your eye on the reward! Keep your eye on the benefits of why the breakthrough is crucial. The sacrifice, hard work, late nights, and tiredness will be worth it. Good things not only come to those who wait (as the saying goes) but also to those who persist and never give up.

*Commit your way to the lord, Trust in him, and he shall bring it to pass.* **Psalm 37:5**

# Three Ways Not to Live Your Life

Life is a precious, unique gift given to us by the Living God. He has designed each of us with a purpose to fulfil. Yet, many people struggle to live life successfully, because instead of discovering their own purpose, they unknowingly live through other factors.

I've observed three common ways in which people live their lives for others. Through others' wishes and desires: Some people hand over the most precious gift, *their life,* to please someone else. For example, some parents try to live out their unfulfilled childhood dreams through their children. They didn't achieve popularity or success, so they sign their child up for activities that garner attention. To them, it feels like validation: *If I couldn't do it, at least my child did.* But the dream belongs to the parent, not the child, therefore robbing the child of their unique purpose and God-given assignment. Living with regret is one of the saddest ways to live. People mourn opportunities missed, time lost, or memories of what *once was.* Every reflection becomes a reminder of what can never be regained. Unknowingly, people disempower themselves because they give away the essence of their lives to others or circumstances that distract them from discovering their true purpose. Living someone else's dream, chasing validation, or dwelling on regrets only steals more time and joy from the present.

The truth is, you are not living your life when you're trying to please others, holding onto the past, or giving others power over your life. It is not too late to start living for yourself. If any of these situations resonate or sound familiar to you, know that it's never too late to take back control of your life. Here is how you can start to do it:

**Seek God for Guidance**

The best way to discover how to live your life is to ask your Creator. *God promises wisdom to those who ask (James 1:5).* If you feel lost, seek Him for guidance, direction, and purpose.

**Discover What You Enjoy**

Start a journey of self-discovery to explore what you enjoy. It may involve trial and error, and that is okay. Reflect on what excites you: What piques your interest? What brings a smile to your face? What have you always wanted to try? Even if you've never considered exploring new things, finding things you enjoy will help you to take control of your life on your journey to living for yourself.

## Own Your Choices and Decisions

A lack of confidence or self-esteem often allows others to influence your decisions. It takes courage to own your choices even when others don't agree. For years, I struggled with this, particularly in my early twenties. Over time, through making mistakes and making my own decisions, I grew in confidence and learned to trust myself. Remember, this is your life. The same grace that others give themselves to grow from their choices and mistakes, you must give yourself as well.

Don't let the fear of mistakes, missed opportunities, or others' opinions hold you back. As long as you have life, you have the opportunity to learn, grow, and move forward. To live your life is true empowerment.

*I will show you great and mighty things you don't know.* **(Jeremiah 33:3)**

# Thrive Not Survive

The older we get, 'thriving' can feel hard to achieve when life and its challenges have you just 'surviving'. Life after 40 is not a time to fade into the background. It's an opportunity to step into your power and thrive. Many older women feel they are at a crossroads, whether due to career shifts, changing family dynamics, or personal issues. But this stage of life is not about surviving; it's about embracing growth, confidence, and fulfilment. I want to share with you six tips to thrive, not just survive. I feel optimistic about the possible opportunities life has in store, and I'm not aiming to just survive; I want to thrive.

## Prioritise Self-Care Without Guilt

As women, we often put others first, but prioritising your well-being is essential. Self-care is not selfish, it's necessary. Whether scheduling regular health check-ups, indulging in a hobby, or simply taking quiet time for yourself, embrace self-care as a non-negotiable part of your life.

## Cultivate a Growth Mindset

Your later years are the perfect time to challenge limiting beliefs. Learning never stops, and whatever decade of life you are in , it can be a great opportunity to take up new skills, start a business, or pursue a long-forgotten passion. Stay curious and open to new experiences. Let personal development be your secret power.

**Strengthen Your Body and Mind**

I love intermittent fasting, walking 10k steps daily, eating healthy (for the most part!) and taking my vitamins. Staying active is key to feeling vibrant. Whether it's Pilates, strength training, or dancing, movement keeps you strong and energised. Equally important is mental well-being. Spending quiet time, praying, meditating, or journaling will help you to maintain emotional balance, and both contribute to a strengthened mind and body.

**Surround Yourself with Positivity**

The people you spend time with impact your energy and mindset. Seek relationships that uplift and inspire you. Let go of toxic connections and invest in friendships that bring joy and support.

**Define Your Success**

You need to redefine what success means to you. Whether it's career growth, financial independence, or personal fulfilment, set goals that align with your values and aspirations. Don't compare your journey to others. Make your path uniquely yours.

**Celebrate Yourself**

Acknowledge and celebrate your achievements. Confidence grows when you recognise your worth and the things you've been able to achieve. Embrace your journey with gratitude and joy. Celebrate your milestones.

Thriving is about embracing life with purpose, confidence, and excitement. Step boldly into each day of life you've been blessed with. You deserve to thrive, not just survive.

*The righteous flourish like the palm tree and grow like a cedar in Lebanon.* **Psalm 92:12**

# Thoughts Become Things

What are you thinking about?

Most of the time, we do not give much thought to what we allow to enter our minds. Life happens, and the influx of images, voices, opinions, and views can influence us subconsciously. On a deeper level, our early life experiences and the things we were told by those regarded as most important to us can not only positively or negatively impact our thoughts but also the course our life takes. A lot of things I was told in childhood by my dad and his actions towards me through sexual abuse had a negative impact on my mind. It was only years later, through CBT (Cognitive Behavioural Therapy), that I learned how my negative thought patterns were influencing my life and how the words spoken to me at an early age affected how I thought about things later on. I call this my 'thought life'.

Until you deal with your negative thoughts, it will be very difficult for you to believe you can become exceptional and not expected. Whether you believe it or not, your thoughts influence the outcomes you are currently experiencing. Thoughts become things, whether good or bad, positive or negative. However, you can empower your mind by giving it new information to influence positive new thoughts. For starters, you can listen to episode 089 of my podcast Living the Empowered Life called: 'break these mindsets' to help you identify areas of your 'thought life' to work on. Other things that can help you in your thought life are:

## Pay attention to what you are thinking about

Get into the habit of monitoring your thoughts. Pay attention to what you listen to and what you watch. Purposefully infuse your mind with things that create an atmosphere of positivity in your mind. There are lots of books, videos, the bible, and therapy services that can help with mindset challenges.

## Swap negative thoughts for positive ones

This is very hard to do, especially if you have allowed negative thoughts to dominate your mind and life for a long time. I allowed negative thoughts to be part of my life for so long, I thought it was just my natural way of thinking, I thought it was normal! A way in which negative thoughts would manifest themselves in my life is through how I viewed myself and the words that came out of my mouth. It was a slow process, but I had to learn to say positive things about myself and when those thoughts tried to creep in, shut them down immediately by deliberately thinking positive thoughts. It may seem tiresome at first, but once you make it a habit, it will get easier.

Believe the best about yourself and be optimistic about your life. Despite what you may feel about yourself or your current circumstances, when you work on your thought life, you will experience a better view of yourself and your capabilities.

*Finally, brothers and sisters, whatever is true, whatever is noble, whatever is right, whatever is pure, whatever is lovely, whatever is admirable—if anything is excellent or praiseworthy—think about such things.* **Philippians 4:8**

# Too Much Education

I know this is going to sound weird, but I think many people suffer from TME…too much education. That sounds crazy, right? Because you know, you can never have enough education and knowledge-especially in an ever-changing world. However, what if I told you, it is a problem if you never use it?

I've had some weird thoughts about this subject, which triggered me to write this book entry. I sometimes wonder when I get emails from people who have loads of letters after their name if they ever use those qualifications they worked hard to obtain (I know my mind ponders the strangest things). Also, when I looked at my framed certificates that hang on my office wall, I realised some of the qualifications I worked so hard to achieve, I have hardly used at all. This realisation caused me to have a period of reflection and evaluation about how I was using my educational achievements.

My educational journey has been up and down. I progressed through my educational milestones up until 1990, at 14 years old, when I was expelled from secondary school for unmanageable behaviour (what can I tell you, the effects of childhood sexual abuse leave you not knowing how to act). From that moment on, the educational roller coaster ride began. I had only been in care a few months, and with each new foster home or children's home came a new education establishment for me to get acquainted with. Individual tuition, small class environment, and a spell of non-existent educational programs in one facility meant I spent most of my days colouring in pictures from a colouring book (hardly stimulating for a young girl who had dreams of being a banker). I was surprised that I left the care system with only an A+ GCSE in English to my name.

After leaving care in 1993 at 17, now a single mum with a baby, I got most of my education through working various retail jobs. I put what I learned to good use. Fast forward to 2015, and I went through a phase where I was addicted to doing short courses. I felt education-starved. Even though I recognised through time that I was able to utilise my skills, talents, and experiences to turn them into opportunities or leverage them to help me advance in life, I still felt I needed to pursue the educational avenue. Maybe subconsciously, my lack of educational achievement in care was a driving factor. The education pinnacle for me came in February 2024 when I achieved my master's degree in entrepreneurship and innovation management. Studying for a degree was never an aspiration when I was young. However, it was my passion for ideas and being a business owner that made me curious about wanting to learn the theoretical side of entrepreneurship.

Education comes through many things, life, experiences, workshops, and courses, to name a few. I realised whether taught or learned, my educational attainment has helped me in my business and charitable endeavours. All the jobs I have had have given me key skills needed for life and business. After deeper reflection, it is not that I have too much education. Rather, in some circumstances, it was not the time to use that qualification. Currently, I use my education, experiences and talents combined with God given wisdom in the things God has called me to do. I believe it has been for such a time as this in my life. Nothing I have done will go to waste.

I have discovered the key to avoiding TME is to use your education in line with things that you are interested in and passionate about. For instance, if you are doing a college course just because it is free, but you have no interest in pursuing a career in that area of study, then it is useless. This is where the journey of too much education starts. Because without a clear purpose of how it will be used, it can trigger a repetitive cycle of accumulating certificates, diplomas, and degrees that you won't use. If you want to avoid too much education or you have realised you have done little to nothing with the qualifications you have, here are some things to help you get the most out of your educational achievements:

**Why do you do it in the first place**

Think about what sparked your interest in the educational course in the first place (passion, deeper learning, private interest). Ask yourself, do you want to become knowledgeable about a subject? What is the end goal for your educational pursuit?

**Evaluate your educational achievement**

If you have educational achievements, what have you not used? (I suggest you write a list). Think about why that is. Is there a way to make use of it now? Can you use it to propel your dreams or as a tool to help you achieve your goals?

**Change your thinking towards your educational achievement**

Think of it as self-investment and personal development, an investment towards your future. Education, if used strategically, can be an asset on your journey to being exceptional not expected. When you reframe your mindset to believe education is a tool to empower you and take you towards your goals or life purpose, you will see its value more than collecting certificates or letters after your name.

*And He said, "Go, and tell this people: 'Keep on hearing, but do not understand; Keep on seeing, but do not perceive.'* **Isaiah 6:9-10**

# There Is a Process To Progress

*YEME Empowerment*

# Quality of Life Is the New Currency

For far too long, we have been fed a message by society that money, status, and a host of other acquired things, is the currency needed to live the life we want. However, many people have found the price to pay for these things has not fulfilled the expectations they had hoped for. Instead, they feel empty and unsatisfied. Over my journey of discovery and continuously seeking to live an empowered life, I have found the quality of life is not found in things (even though financial resources can make things a bit easier), it is found in what you do with what you already have. Quality of life IS the new currency. Not money, not things, not validation of others, or titles. Here is how you build the quality currency into your life:

## Enjoy life doing things you love

What do you love to do? Start doing it! Spend as much time as you can doing the things that make you happy. Even if it is only once a month, at least that is time spent adding quality to your life. Explore the possibilities and opportunities life has to offer, and have the courage to try new things.

## Spend quality time with yourself and people you love

More real-life interactions, less time on social media. Spend time getting to know yourself and see how doing it helps you improve yourself. Also, if you have good people around you, invest time in their company. Good conversation and interactions never go amiss!

## Invest in quality currency

Trade peace for stress. Live life for you and not for others. You do not need money, status, or any other thing to have quality of life (you'd be surprised how many people start from a point of 'I need money to'). Today, I encourage you to invest in adding quality currency to your life. Remember, time is not something you can get back, so invest your currency wisely.

*Whereas you do not know what will happen tomorrow. For what is your life? It is even a vapour that appears for a little time and vanishes away.* **James 4:14**

# What the Eighties Taught Me

From listening to Absolute Eighties Radio, following nostalgia accounts on Twitter (now X), and in general, my love for this wonderful decade, inspired me to think about what the eighties taught me. Life was carefree then. If you are a Generation X baby, you know what I am talking about! Back then, I lived on a council estate in Battersea, South London, and so did most of my friends. The memories I have of this time are special, and they have formed some of the happiest times in my life. Pop music, jelly shoes, The A Team, sitcoms such the Golden Girls, playing out with friends, hopscotch, group dancing, metropolitan police disco, school dinners, dressing up, leg warmers, neon clothing, McDonalds, snowball and baby cham, penny sweets, jubilees, slush puppy, Opal Fruits, Rainbow Brite, Cabbage Patch dolls, Smurfs, Rainbow, Karate Kid, Ghostbusters, Desperately Seeking Susan, Pretty In Pink, Knight Rider, The Fall Guy, Magnum, Saturday morning TV, Mannequin, Dallas, Worzel Gummage, EastEnders, Rubik's cube, Speak and Spell. So many memories, I could go on and on... the eighties were special.

The reason I selected this decade to share with you, is because it was a complex time in my life. As previously mentioned, I experienced childhood sexual abuse, which happened in the mid-eighties (from the of age nine to thirteen years old). The trauma could have left me with a long-lasting negative impression and outlook about that time in my life. However, after overcoming much adversity and reflecting on this period of my life retrospectively, I have gained a newfound appreciation. I do not look back with regret, but to glean from that time, things to enrich and empower me on my exceptional not expected journey. My early positive experiences of the eighties planted the seeds and laid the foundation for the life I live today. So let me share with you what the eighties taught me:

**Fun and laughter keeps you young**

The eighties taught me to be carefree, laugh, and have fun. To enjoy the day you're blessed with rather than worrying about the day you have not yet been given tomorrow. You know, as we get older, we can become rigid. Age has a way of convincing us that being silly and carefree is for the young, and as those days are behind us, we need to become "serious adults". Of course, there is a time and place for everything. However, age should not be a closed door that prevents you or me from enjoying life.

## That imagination is priceless

In the eighties there was no internet, computers, or mobile phones to keep us occupied (late eighties those luxuries were reserved for the yuppie types). As children we had to use our imagination to think creatively to make up games and keep ourselves occupied. The eighties taught me that if I want something I can make it happen. That is why I believe I am drawn to being an entrepreneur. Everything I have created through my businesses has been achieved using creative imagination. The eighties' imagination is about thinking big and finding solutions. If we did not have it or our parents couldn't afford it, we had to use imagination to create other means.

## Life is what you make it

1985 onwards was not a particularly great time in my life because that is when my abuse started. However, even though I went through a difficult time, I still tried to make the most of my life. Even now the fact I remember the fun things of the eighties; the lessons, the laughs and the good memories is unbelievable. This has helped me to enjoy and make the most of my life now.

**Less is more**

We never had everything we wanted growing up, my brother, sister, and I, but we had what we needed and made much of what we had. Lovely meals prepared by my mum, receiving the present I circled in the catalogue at Christmas, and family, friends, and life; I had a lot. Even if I could not have something, I may have had a sulk, but I got over it.

In this social media, consumer crazy, technology driven age that we live in now, the simplicity and beauty of less is more is gone. That is why simplicity YouTube channels have amassed millions of followers because their content is anti-overindulgence. Consumerism has become the modern-day poison in which I have regrettably partaken. However, I have started to make changes. Unsubscribing from emails sent by fashion and lifestyle companies, selling stuff I no longer use, becoming aware of the emotional triggers that influence me to buy stuff, and pausing and questioning internally why I want to buy something. I am a work in progress, and it is a journey of unlearning habits. FOMO (fear of missing out) is only a thing if you let it be. Patience, simplicity, and appreciating not accumulating more is one of the major things the eighties taught me.

## To have an open mind

As they say, variety is the spice of life. In the eighties, I had friends who were of a different race and culture to me. I loved reggae, funk, and soul music, commonly associated and liked within my culture, but I also liked pop, nu romance, and jazz. I jumped off roofs with my friends, played new and different games, and took part in different lessons in school. And I enjoyed all of it. Keeping an open mind helped me later in life to develop confidence, take opportunities, and try new experiences.

I am grateful for such a wonderful time in my life, the good, the bad, and the difficult; the eighties helped me become the woman I am today. I want to encourage you to look at a past era of your life and think about what it taught you. Our past experiences play a part in shaping our thinking, influencing motivations, and contributing to building skills and talents, and teach us lessons about things we may or may not take forward in life.

*"Rejoice always, pray without ceasing, give thanks in all circumstances; for this is the will of God in Christ Jesus for you."* **1 Thessalonians 5:16-18**

# Where You Go You Grow

I came across something both surprising and logical. A survey conducted by neuroscientists at MIT revealed that motivation tends to decrease with age. As we grow older, it appears that maintaining a driven, growth mindset becomes more challenging.

Yes, it is true that pursuing growth can become increasingly challenging as we age. This happens for various reasons. Many people are settled into their comfort zones, neglecting the practices that once fuelled their development. Factors like established habits, a reluctance to step outside familiar routines, a shortage of time, and a lack of energy can all contribute to stagnation.

As a certified empowerment coach dedicated to helping individuals embrace change later in life, and as someone who began my journey towards an empowered life at thirty-five, I believe one significant factor can help overcome age-related challenges: individual motivation. It is the thing that naturally stimulates growth. Personal motivation is deeply rooted in our desires, hopes, and dreams. It's the driving force that pushes us to step outside our comfort zone and explore new possibilities, even when past experiences have been unsuccessful. Even if these goals and aspirations have been set aside for a while, motivation reignites the desire to pursue them and encourages us to give them another shot.

However, here's what you need to understand: growth happens when you go. You must use that motivation to step outside your comfort zone and rekindle those forgotten hopes and dreams. It demands energy, sacrifice, and time. And here's a surprise for some: it doesn't just happen because you get older. It requires focused, intentional effort to include it in your life as you get older.

So, with all that said, I want to encourage you to grow. You can start your journey by:

**Spending time reflecting on what area of your life growth has stagnated in**

Life has a way of shifting our focus, making it easy to overlook things we once deemed important. This might include dreams you had, projects you hoped to begin, or even those you started but never completed. You may already recognise a part of you that is neglected. It's essential to understand the reasons behind this so you can address and overcome them. Self-reflection, where you thoughtfully assess your life, is a powerful tool for breaking free from stagnation and moving towards growth.

## Chase growth

Invest some of your time doing new things. Change your habits. Disrupt your routine. Anything that stimulates growth is good for you. You can start with small things, and once you've got into the rhythm of growth activities, you can pick up the pace. Pursue growth and learn to love it!

## Grow and glow

When you recognise growth, celebrate it! As an empowered lifer, this is a must. Remember the study I referred to at the beginning? It basically said that age is an enemy to our motivation to do something new. Well, that is even more reason to celebrate that new or different thing you have done. In doing so, you will add a vibrancy and glow to your life that may inspire you to pursue even more opportunities for growth.

Remember—growth isn't confined to your past; it extends into your future. It thrives in life's uncertainties. Don't fear the unknown, embrace it. Each day offers a chance to evolve into the person you've always aspired to be.

*Practice these things, and immerse yourself in them, so that all may see your progress.* **1 Timothy 4:15**

# While You're Waiting, You're Wasting Time

Do you know one of the common assumptions people make about time? It is that they have all the time in the world! Many people put things off until tomorrow what they can do today; after all, the thing they're supposed to do is not going anywhere. But in my experience, putting things off and not actioning the task at hand in a prompt manner only enables a spirit of procrastination. I get it. You want to feel in the mood to focus, to feel ready to put in the work to follow your dream or do that thing you have always wanted to do. Unfortunately, achieving things in life does not wait for you to 'feel' like doing it, and certainty there is no perfect time.

Time waits for no one. While you are waiting for the perfect time, circumstances, situation, or opportunity, time is passing you by. What you want is not going to drop into your lap. No one is going to bring it to you or point you to where it is. You must get motivated to get it. Staying in your comfort zone, hoping somehow what you want will find you, is not going to happen. Therefore, you must start working towards what you want. Use your time to order your steps. The saying 'time is of the essence' is true. You can make the most of time by:

## Figure out your true goals and desires

One of the most important things that is going to hopefully motivate you to stop wasting time is considering the things that matter to you the most. If you could spend your life doing this thing, what would it be? A big factor in time-wasting is not being sure of what to focus your time on. Once you figure that out, thinking about how to spend time engaging in it will make the task of planning the time for it easier.

## Making the most of your day

You can do this by planning your day beforehand to maximise it. What I find effective in helping me to plan my day is a dated planner. I spend ten to fifteen minutes the night before, checking my planner and adding any action points for tasks to complete. It is also time to check on anything outstanding to finish. In planning your day, you are creating an awareness of what needs to be accomplished in it.

## Confront your time-waster

What is that thing that is wasting your time? Is it fear? Is it that you are not sure what to do? Is it that you lack courage? Unless you confront the thing that causes you to waste your time, you will not get any closer to completing the things you keep putting off.

You need to consider whether time-wasting over that thing is worth it. Confront it and seek out solutions to overcome it. To be blessed with another day means you have been extended and gifted time to do things that matter. Don't wait and waste it. Make each day count.

*To everything there is a season, A time for every purpose under heaven.* **Ecclesiastes 3:1**

# You Are Good Enough

Imposter syndrome and inferiority complex are real struggles. Feeling unworthy or not good enough to seize opportunities or pursue ambitions we believe are meant for more "qualified" and "deserving" people is something many of us experience daily. I've faced these feelings countless times, especially when I face new situations. Even while earning my degree, I battled imposter syndrome. But the moment I recognised those thoughts, I had to shut them down. I reminded myself that I am just as worthy and capable as anyone else pursuing a master's degree.

As you near the end of this book, I want to remind you: you are good enough. You are no less than anyone else in whatever you choose to do in life. Don't let a job, relationship, the size of your dream, your emotions, or even other people make you feel otherwise. And most importantly, don't let negative self-talk convince you that you are anything less than valuable and worthy. In God's eyes, you are precious, and nothing in this world can change that. Don't let life intimidate you. Step forward with courage and explore all the opportunities life presents to you.

*For God has not given us a spirit of fear, but of power and of love and of a sound mind.* **2 Timothy 1:7**

# You Can't Avoid the "Icks" of Life

You may be wondering: what is an ick? According to the Cambridge dictionary, an ick is: used to express *a feeling of shock or dislike that makes you feel sick.* Words and phrases related to the word ick include repel, dread, and dislike. There are many things individual to each of us that we could say give us the 'ick'. Failure, being told no, being uncomfortable, the possibility of rejection, unpleasant people, situations, or conversations. Some people think if they avoid things, ignore them, bury their head in the sand so to speak, or pretend whatever it is does not exist, it will go away. However, the truth is these life-stances (as I like to call them) are integrated into the fabric of life. They are very much a part of life, as breathing and all the other parts of life we don't dismiss (good times, nice times, pleasant people). There is no getting away from it: you can't avoid the icks of life.

One of my biggest icks that made me feel so uncomfortable was facing the ugly truth of my childhood abuse. For many years, I tried to suppress dealing with it by using avoidance tactics and vices (smoking weed, drinking) to avoid thinking about it at all. However, memories, people, feelings, and even certain smells reminded me that I had to face my ick, otherwise my life would continue in a repetitive cycle of self-sabotage and stagnancy. Unfortunately, it took a mental breakdown at twenty-two years old to face my ick, and it was horrible. I felt sick, angry, and sad. However, finally confronting my 'icks' set me free from the feelings of guilt, shame, and secrecy. After doing the hard work of therapy, I gained a different perspective on my ick; that I was indeed strong to have survived the very things that made me dislike myself.

Here is what I learned about icks:

## Accept that icks are part of life

The no's, the mistakes, the failures, the unpleasantness. Once you can accept them, you will start to learn different ways to deal with them. That difficult situation? seek advice. Hard to accept, no? accept that it is not time for the yes. Fear rejection? remember, rejection is preparation for the very thing you are going to get. Moreover, it builds resilience.

## Icks are character building

Icks prepare you for bigger icks in life. The very situations, people, or things you don't like are there to teach you something to develop or prepare you for something in the future.

## Not everything is an ick

Sometimes, the things you assume are icks are not at all. As humans, we have a habit of rejecting things we don't like. If you want to live an exceptional not expected life, it will require you to deal with things you don't like and any Icks that come your way. You have to confront the unpleasantness; don't avoid it.

*My brethren, count it all joy when you fall into various trials, knowing that the testing of your faith produces patience. But let patience have its perfect work, that you may be perfect and complete, lacking nothing.* **James 1: 2-5.**

# You've Got to Want It More

The day you want more for yourself than the "less" you are living with, is the day you decide it's time for a change. What is the "less" you are settling for? Sometimes, when we don't have people around us to encourage us to be ambitious and audacious about the things we want, it is easy to settle for less. I used to struggle with believing big. I remember a few times when I openly voiced that I wanted to achieve big things. At one time I was working in a toxic workplace with dreams to start my own business doing the things I loved. You can imagine the looks and responses I got from some of my colleagues. They probably thought it was wishful thinking on my part. After all, wasn't I sitting in an office like them doing a job I didn't particularly like? However, after being fed up with the lack of progression on the traditional career path, I finally had the courage to act; I left my job without another to go to. I decided the time was now or never to start my business. That was seven years ago.

You see, after much mental back and forth, I wanted the freedom to follow my heart's desire to create an empowerment company. I wanted it more than job stability. I wanted to experience doing things that I loved. That mattered more than anything. What do you want to experience more of in your life? Is it to turn that side hustle into a business? Is it spending time developing the things you are passionate about? Is it to enjoy life at your own pace? No one can want it for you. You have got to want it for yourself. And you know, it is totally possible to get what you want; you have the desire, you just need the courage and motivation to go for it. Once you have these two things and you act, those lesser things won't have the appeal they once had. So, to help you on your 'want it more' journey, here are some starting steps:

## Decide what you want

When deciding what you want you will be more inclined to focus. Once your mind is made up to go after the thing you want more, regardless of the cost, that is one of the biggest steps to take.

## Make a plan

Now it is time to make a plan. Remember, you might not achieve your goal or dream overnight. However, having a plan of the steps you need to take will encourage you on your journey. When you plan, include small steps as they will motivate you and celebrate achieving your milestones.

**Keep a reminder of what the 'more' will mean for your life**

Not only will it keep you focused and motivated, it will remind you why you need to exchange the less you've settled with, for the more you desire. Write it, draw it, keep it close to you to remind you.

And to add the icing to the cake, if you bring your plans to the Lord God, He will guide your plans in alignment with His will for your life and establish your path. Remember, you are created for more, so go for it!

*Delight yourself also in the Lord, And He shall give you the desires of your heart.* **Psalm 37:4**

# You Belong

Have you ever been somewhere that made you feel you didn't quite belong? I remember many years back when stepping into high-end clothing stores felt intimidating. I couldn't afford those beautiful pieces, but I still enjoyed browsing. Sadly, the sales assistants sometimes made it obvious that I didn't fit the image of their typical customer, leaving me feeling uncomfortable and out of place. Over time, though, I've gained confidence and grown personally; no longer do I let others' attitudes dictate where I should or shouldn't go.

Over the years, I've visited many places where, based on certain demographics, people might think "I don't belong". For example, at the Antiquarian Book Fair held at the Saatchi Gallery, I found myself as the only Black woman among a predominantly upper-class, white crowd. Though I may have seemed out of place, I knew I belonged just as much as anyone else because of my shared love for books. Similarly, during a visit to the Battersea Affordable Art Fair, I was one of only two Black people among the artsy, middle-class white attendees.

While enjoying a glass of prosecco at the bar, I struck up a conversation with the bar hostess. Out of curiosity, I asked, "Have you seen many Black visitors at this event?" Her answer was telling: "No. At last night's opening, there was only one Black person." Together, we speculated on why that might be, concluding from her perspective as a young white woman and mine as a Black attendee that: "Maybe they feel they don't belong".

This may be true, as black artists have indeed organised similar events for their communities. But my point is that what truly matters isn't someone's outward appearance. How you look shouldn't prevent you from exploring places you may not usually visit. You belong there simply because you're interested. Your passion, curiosity, or love for the subject is what qualifies you. Everything else is secondary. The only way you exclude yourself is by choosing not to go, influenced by insecurities you think others might have about you being there.

One powerful catalyst for growth is breaking free from the familiar. Stepping beyond the limits of your usual routine and immersing yourself in motivational and inspirational environments influences life change. This disruption of habit and mindset creates space for exciting life transformations.

Visiting unfamiliar places broadens my perspective, revealing creative possibilities and new opportunities for learning. It has deepened my appreciation for aspects of life I might never have encountered. Through these experiences, I've gained insights into art, architecture, and people, all of which have enriched my life in countless ways and helped me to develop courage.

Is there a place you've always dreamed of visiting but felt you'd stick out like a sore thumb? I encourage you to go anyway; you might be surprised by the experience. Is it the theatre? Having afternoon tea at an upmarket hotel? Or maybe visiting a prestigious art gallery? My next goal is to attend the ballet at the Royal Opera House in Covent Garden (which I achieved). Keep these things in mind as you step into your new adventure:

## You belong

It's as simple as that. Nothing can disqualify you from what truly matters to *you*. Hold on to that.

## Embrace the experience

Sure, you might get a few curious looks as I did, but let those go. You're there to enjoy yourself. Enjoy the experience and ignore people's looks.

## Embrace discomfort

Visiting places where you feel out of place can be a powerful catalyst for personal growth. Stepping outside your comfort zone challenges you. Although it may feel strange at first, it can be just what you need to bring fresh energy and perspective into your life. Make a habit of seeking out these moments. Try doing the opposite of what you usually do, and let discomfort become part of your routine for growth.

Don't count yourself out of anything in life. You are just as deserving as anyone else to embrace everything life has to offer.

*Whenever I am afraid, I will trust in You. In God I have put my trust; I will not fear. What can flesh do to me?* **Psalm 56:3-4**

Do you need a courageous action plan to achieve your goals and dreams? Check out The Courage Course on Thinkific.com

https://theempoweredlife-ad5c.thinkific.com/courses/the-courage-course

Social media:
YouTube – Living the Empowered Life
Instagram – Yeme_Empowerment
Twitter – Yeme Empowerment
Facebook – Yeme Empowerment
Tik Tok – yeme_empowerment22

Visit www.yemeempowerment.com to see what services and resources we offer for solutions to your current challenges.

Also, you can check out the Living the Empowered Life Podcast on Apple iTunes, Stitcher, and Spotify.

Get in touch. I would love to connect with you!